Teaching

one Pagers

Evidence-informed summaries for busy educational professionals

Jamie Clark

JOHN CATT
FROM HODDER EDUCATION

Hachette UK's policy is to use papers that are natural, renewable and recyclable products and made from wood grown in well-managed forests and other controlled sources. The logging and manufacturing processes are expected to conform to the environmental regulations of the country of origin.

Orders: please contact Hachette UK Distribution, Hely Hutchinson Centre, Milton Road, Didcot, Oxfordshire, OX11 7HH. Telephone: +44 (0)1235 827827. Email education@hachette.co.uk. Lines are open from 9 a.m. to 5 p.m., Monday to Friday.

ISBN: 9781398388659

© Jamie Clark 2024

First published in 2024 by
John Catt from Hodder Education,
An Hachette UK Company
15 Riduna Park, Station Road,
Melton, Woodbridge IP12 1QT
Telephone: +44 (0)1394 389850
www.johncatt.com

A catalogue record for this title is available from the British Library

Typeset by John Catt Educational Limited
Front Cover Designed by Jamie Clark
Printed and bound in Great Britain by Bell and Bain Ltd, Glasgow

Testimonials

MARY MYATT
@MaryMyatt

Teaching One-Pagers would have been so helpful to me earlier in my career; it was all pretty hit and miss! These summaries of what we currently understand as the most important and efficient ways to improve outcomes will act both as an aide-mémoire for those who have already delved into these fields and a gateway for those who are new to this work. It's hard to distil this information and to capture the kernels. A great boon for the profession.

KATE JONES
@KateJones_teach

This is a terrific book! A great addition to any PD library. Jamie has included an impressive amount in terms of the content, and has done so with concise, clear and incredibly helpful explanations. *Teaching One-Pagers* can be used to support individual teachers' development, as part of professional dialogue amongst a department, or even to help ensure consistency across a whole school. An insightful, informative and interesting read.

PEPS MCCREA
@PepsMccrea

Jamie's *Teaching One-Pagers* serves up tasty tapas of current thinking, expertly blending an insightful array of evidence-informed ideas with a visually scrumptious presentation, perfect for tantalising that educational appetite.

OLLIE LOVELL
@ollie_lovell

BRADLEY BUSCH
@BradleyKBusch

SARAH COTTINGHATT
@SCottinghatt

More and more teachers around the world are taking the time and expending the effort to truly develop their own expertise in teaching. Jamie Clark has done this excellently in this book; his clear and powerful illustrations are the icing on the cake of his wonderful work. I commend Jamie on *Teaching One-Pagers* without reservation and encourage more teachers to make teaching their own and truly master the profession through reviewing wonderful resources like this one.

Teaching One-Pagers is an incredible idea. It is a great answer to the tricky question of 'how do you best help information-hungry but time-poor teachers access the latest and greatest ideas on teaching?' What Jamie does is quite special, as not only does he highlight key concepts, but also where people can go next to find out more. The graphics in this book are gorgeous. The content is evidence-based and the strategies are insightful. I can't recommend this book enough!

The one-pagers are our route into the research. Jamie has done an excellent job of creating a really simple and satisfying way to get a sense of a topic, which we can use as a springboard for discussion and to dig deeper. By organising the book into three strands, its easy to navigate and utilise to build our understanding of key ideas. I've enjoyed these one-pages for a long time and it's great to have them all in one place!

JADE PEARCE
@PearceMrs

JIM KNIGHT
@jimknight99

ALEX QUIGLEY
@AlexJQuigley

This book is a game changer for anyone who wants to quickly improve their knowledge of evidence-informed practice, or for any early career teachers. Jamie succinctly distils complex ideas into one-page summaries that are easy to understand and digest. One-pagers are ideal for sharing with teachers across your school, for use in staff CPD, and as discussion prompts in staff meetings. This book makes essential reading for all teachers and is extremely beneficial to T&L or CPD leads.

Teaching One-Pagers is a great tool for anyone looking to learn and reflect on their teaching skills in a short amount of time. The way Jamie takes different ideas and approaches and visually captures what it is and how you can apply it is brilliant. This is a great book for any teacher wanting access to evidence-based practices at the ready.

Education is undoubtedly brilliant, but for busy teachers there can be a dizzying array of advice, theory, strategies and research to digest. Clark's one-pagers offer a cleverly distilled and easily digestible approach to a superb array of principles and practices drawn from edu-research. The book is easy to read and use and offers a great starting point for time-poor teachers seeking to engage with reflective reading on improving their craft.

DYLAN WILIAM
@dylanwiliam

Teachers have never had better access to educational research, but the sheer volume that is now available is overwhelming and this is why Jamie Clark's *Teaching One-Pagers* is such a wonderful resource. It presents the key findings on a wide range of topics accurately, without oversimplifying, in a well-signposted and easily accessible form. Put simply, if you teach, you need this.

JOHN HATTIE
@john_hattie

Teachers are busy people, so every resource that gets to the big picture quickly is of high value. These 50+ summaries are evidence-based, beautifully presented, and linked to the original works. Jamie Clark has made a major contribution, and this book is a great go-to resource for finding the latest, fastest and best information.

TOM SHERRINGTON
@teacherhead

Without question, Jamie Clark is one of the very best creators of one-page summaries that deliver on all fronts. His one-pagers are stylish, clear and visually engaging; they are well researched and well written and, as a whole, the collection represents a brilliant summary of the most useful ideas for teachers to discuss and focus on. *Teaching One-Pagers* is a unique book that deserves a wide audience and I'm confident that teachers in every setting will love it.

To Lucy, Finley and Evie.
Thanks for putting up with me.
This book is a tribute to the joy you bring into my life.

Acknowledgments

I would like to thank everyone who contributed to the creation of this book. It has been a bumpy ride but your support, encouragement and insights have been crucial in bringing these pages together.

Firstly, I'd like to thank my wife, Lucy, and my children, Finley and Evie, for their patience and support throughout this process. Your love has been a constant source of strength for me.

Special thanks to Oliver Caviglioli for his expert advice and influence on the book's overall design. Oliver's approach to presenting complex ideas in a clear and engaging manner has been a guiding light in my design choices, helping to make the content not just informative but also visually captivating. His generosity in sharing one of his graphics has notably enhanced the book's quality.

To my teacher friends, Johnny Ho, Noel Patterson and Marc Caporn who offered support, constructive feedback and a listening ear, thank you for being great mates and excellent sounding boards. I owe you a few well-earned beers!

I'd also like to thank the amazing educators who gave up their time to read drafts and give me valuable feedback. In particular, Bradley Busch and Mark Dowley – this book is better because of your input.

Lastly, I acknowledge the readers and supporters of my one-pagers. Your interest and engagement online have been the driving force behind this book. I hope you find it insightful and valuable.

Foreword

Tom Sherrington

The appetite for one-pagers amongst teachers has been a fascinating phenomenon in recent years. Every time Jamie Clark posts one of his creations, they quickly fly around the world via social media. Why is this? I think it's an indication of not only how incredibly busy teachers are but also how committed and enthusiastic they are about their all-important work.

If you are keen to learn more about teaching, a high-quality, visually-engaging one-page summary can support you in a number of ways:

WIDER READING	DISCUSSION	SHARED UNDERSTANDING
can act as a...	can provide a...	can provide...
signpost to wider reading, giving you the highlights so you can focus on deeper exploration at a later date.	reminder of something you have already read in detail, stimulating further discussion with colleagues.	prompts for your reflections and PD processes, helping to foster shared understanding of key concepts, problems and solutions.

TOM SHERRINGTON

Jamie is one of the very best creators of one-page summaries that deliver on all fronts.

Without question, Jamie Clark is one of the very best creators of one-page summaries that deliver on all fronts. His one-pagers are well-researched and well-written and, as a whole, the collection represents a brilliant summary of the most useful ideas for teachers to discuss and focus on. *Teaching One-Pagers* is a unique book that deserves a wide audience and I'm confident that teachers in every setting will love it.

Oliver Caviglioli

Jamie Clark is a master curator. He has selected, organised, designed and presented the most relevant, referenced and hotly debated educational texts in recent years. His collection is meaningful, practical and endlessly fascinating.

By assembling the content in this easy to navigate way, Jamie has shared his own schema. His organisation of the content – the selecting, categorising and sequencing – is hidden in plain sight but is a major contribution in providing significance and connections across the pages.

Within each page, Jamie dissects and structures the content with an educator's mind and designer's eye, but don't limit your understanding of design to mere aesthetics. Jamie has presented the material to make our reading both more effective and pleasing. The columns, titles, highlighted sections, call-outs, portraits and diagrams all contribute to our pleasure in understanding.

Given the problem of searching to be ever more evidence-informed while working towards teacher wellbeing in a time-scarce profession, Jamie's book is a highly inventive and welcome solution. Of course, some may critique the easily gained knowledge, deploring the lack of time and dedication sweating over laborious texts. That misses the point. Just look at the comprehensive references at the back and you will be assured that each idea can be followed up in detailed depth.

I welcome Jamie's studious, dedicated and skilful application of his reading for the benefit of the teaching community. It is generous and deserves universal acclaim.

OLIVER CAVIGLIOLI

Jamie has presented the material to make our reading both more effective and pleasing. The columns, the titles, the highlighted sections, the call-outs, the portraits and the diagrams all contribute to our pleasure in understanding.

Tom Sherrington is a bestselling author, popular blogger and educational consultant with over 30 years of experience as a teacher and school leader. Oliver Caviglioli, with a decade of experience as a special school headteacher, is a globally renowned educational information designer. Together, they are the creators of the groundbreaking Teaching WalkThrus series, a vital resource for educators seeking to enhance their pedagogical knowledge and improve their teaching practice.

Contents

This book is organised into three main collections:

Collection 1: Learning and Memory
Collection 2: Expert Teaching Principles
Collection 3: Classroom Culture

Teaching one Pagers

Introduction

Back in 2009, completing my teaching degree was one of the hardest things I had ever accomplished. That was what I thought at the time at least. My first year of teaching was the real hard task.

I felt like a fish out of water – designing my own lessons, sometimes winging it when a lesson went wrong and redirection was needed, and not always knowing if lessons were having an impact. Where were the tutors who would answer an email within 24 hours? Where were the 'good lesson' rubrics and checklists that I could tick off? Gone were the days of near-instant feedback and endless paperwork that reassured me that I was doing things right. Typically, other members of staff were busy and inaccessible. The long-term plans and schemes of work may as well have been blueprints for a new space station. Worst of all, the students were unpredictable. The best lesson in the world didn't always result in row upon row of smiling, engaged students completing grade A work. There were puzzled frowns, complaints of 'I don't understand', and even some downright disrespect. I consulted my piles of university notes but they seemed as much use as a roll of toilet paper. To be frank, toilet paper would have been of more use at this point!

My mentor, Sue Hynes, was a wonderful, caring woman and an exceptional teacher. I'm only a casual acquaintance of *Star Wars* but I can't help but think of Sue as the Yoda to my Luke – the wise, trustworthy adviser in charge of a keen yet naive novice. Old school to a fault, Sue gave me some of the best advice in my first year. For example, she rightly explained that 'You learn more from the lessons that go wrong than those that go well'. Sue also took the staunch traditional Yorkshire perspective that folk will get better through hard graft and well-earned experience. This certainly holds water, but when I'd taught a short string of lessons that seemed to strike a chord with only a few of the brighter students, I needed a new approach and wasn't sure where to go or what to do. Experience is great, but the road is long. My limited experience as a novice teacher wasn't exactly varied. I needed some reliable, evidence-informed ideas in the mix as well.

Of course, whole-staff PD days were where we received training on pedagogical practice. Some of it was useful and I remember scrawling notes and stealing the odd PowerPoint, but it's all too common for the 'good stuff' to get lost in a slew of other issues and responsibilities, often the nuts and bolts stuff of the school: budget, timetables, who was using the library that week. When this was combined with my own workload (which, more often than not, felt like an avalanche of marking) and commitments outside of school, a focus on good teaching again slid by the wayside.

Once more, I found myself agonising about what activities I would be doing with my class in order to keep them settled and engaged. I rarely thought about what I actually wanted them to *learn*. This experience chimes with Professor Robert Coe's ideas surrounding his 2014 report, 'What Makes Great Teaching?'. Around that time, Coe outlined a series of 'poor proxies for learning' that, even now, offer a reminder of the pitfalls of focusing too heavily on task completion and student compliance (see the diagram on the next page). Coe's ideas, compounded with the incoming wave of edu-blogs and online networking, helped me change gears and up my game.

Getting involved with the edu-Twitter (now called X) community in 2014 was a game-changer. I felt as if I'd found my tribe. Here were like-minded people from all over the world with a wealth of knowledge and a plethora of ideas. These teachers produced blogs and published books that were purposefully aware of research, such as findings from cognitive science. Though I still cringe at the memory of how much time I spent creating exquisite resources in Microsoft Word (I had yet to learn proper time-management!), the lessons and resources I painstakingly crafted began to improve. Over the years, I have slowly learned that being evidence-informed involves blending insights from various research into teaching methods and constantly assessing the effectiveness of teaching along the way. No more doubling and tripling down on fancy four-part lessons that didn't yield proper results. My teaching gradually became more refined and focused on getting my students to *think* and not just *do*.

PROFESSOR ROBERT COE

I have come up with a simple formulation: learning happens when people have to think hard. (2013)

SUE HYNES

You learn more from the lessons that go wrong than those that go well.

ROBERT COE'S POOR PROXIES FOR LEARNING (2015)

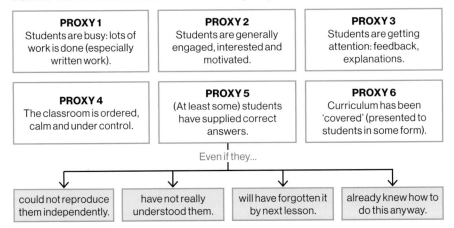

PROXY 1
Students are busy: lots of work is done (especially written work).

PROXY 2
Students are generally engaged, interested and motivated.

PROXY 3
Students are getting attention: feedback, explanations.

PROXY 4
The classroom is ordered, calm and under control.

PROXY 5
(At least some) students have supplied correct answers.

PROXY 6
Curriculum has been 'covered' (presented to students in some form).

Even if they...

could not reproduce them independently.

have not really understood them.

will have forgotten it by next lesson.

already knew how to do this anyway.

In recent years, I started to share my own educational insights and design edu-summaries for colleagues at my school. The end result of this long, sometimes sticky journey is this book of *Teaching One-Pagers* that you hold in your hands. I intend it to be used as an easily accessible go-to when you're feeling uninspired and overwhelmed. It goes back to the bread and butter of good teaching practice – evidence-based teaching without excess fluff or edu-jargon. I expect this book to be something of a working document, with your own annotations scrawled in the margins, or the pages pinned to your staffroom noticeboard as a quick reference. In my own experience, I have found one-pagers to be incredibly useful for making tried and tested ideas readily available. They are designed to inform a coach's feedback meeting, provoke professional conversations and ignite a curiosity to read more, learn new skills and self-improve. In essence, the one-pagers in this book aim to provide busy educators with the following building blocks:

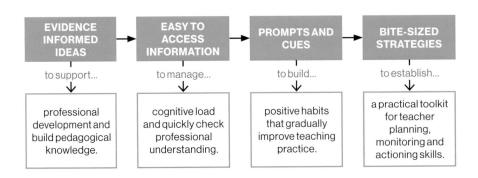

EVIDENCE INFORMED IDEAS	EASY TO ACCESS INFORMATION	PROMPTS AND CUES	BITE-SIZED STRATEGIES
to support...	to manage...	to build...	to establish...
professional development and build pedagogical knowledge.	cognitive load and quickly check professional understanding.	positive habits that gradually improve teaching practice.	a practical toolkit for teacher planning, monitoring and actioning skills.

Research suggests that effective continued professional development (CPD) helps teachers form a common language and shared understanding of what works within a school's context. Having access to a collection of easy-to-implement teaching strategies (as shown in these one-pagers!) is invaluable for developing a shared vision. Jim Knight, founder and senior partner of the Instructional Coaching Group (ICG), refers to collections of strategies as 'instructional playbooks', which are essential because they make learning concrete and easy to access. Knight (2021) believes that the one-pager format functions as an effective 'communication tool coaches can share with teachers and others'.

JIM KNIGHT

Playbooks are essential because they make learning real... the One-Pager functions as a concise communication tool coaches can share with teachers and others. (2021)

Due to their slim, simple nature, one-page summaries are less likely to overload working memory as they focus only on the most relevant information. They give enough for teachers to quickly grasp the main ideas without straining their cognitive processes – let's face it, as teachers, our cognitive processes are strained enough as it is! As Sweller et al (2019) explain, 'Human cognitive processing is heavily constrained by our limited working memory, which can only process a limited number of information elements at a time.' Well-designed one-pagers help teachers better understand the material by layering in multiple examples and chunking information using headings, subheadings and lists. Employing strategies such as dual coding (the combination of verbal and visual instruction) also supports with managing cognitive load. The most effective summaries include visual representations such as diagrams to present ideas or map out teaching sequences. This means they are great for supporting professional development such as workshops or instructional coaching programs.

JOHN SWELLER

Human cognitive processing is heavily constrained by our limited working memory, which can only process a limited number of information elements at a time. (2019)

Excellent research from the Education Endowment Foundation (et al 2021) suggests that the core 'building blocks of professional development' must include the essential 'mechanisms'. The one-pagers in this book include mechanisms from all four of the main groups. The summaries help to: manage cognitive load, revisit prior learning, present credible information, provide instruction and present powerful prompts and cues.

THE EDUCATION ENDOWMENT FOUNDATION'S CPD MECHANISMS

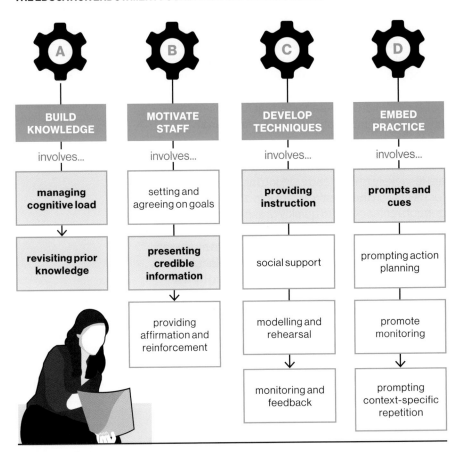

Professional development aside, I don't expect everything you need to know to be included in this book. A common misconception about one-pagers is that they oversimplify complex and nuanced topics. This perspective misses the point. One-pagers are not intended to be the sole sources of information; they are summaries that add clarity to strategies, encourage deeper reading and inspire action. In other words, consider this book to be a 'starting point' if you're a teacher perhaps not *au fait* with cognitive science, or a refresher if you're a teacher who is more well-read. I know there are some of you who read edu-books for fun! The references at the end of the book are for further reading. While I have condensed the information into these one-pagers as accurately as possible, I admit that they may lack the depth that comes across in the full book or research paper. What is more, some of the ideas presented in this book might not work for every student or in every context. It's a case of using your professional judgment. As my old mentor Sue would have said, 'it's a matter of using your common sense!'

In his critically acclaimed book, *Atomic Habits*, author James Clear (2018) explains the tiny steps needed to build healthy habits so that you can achieve more. Clear explains the differences between what he calls, 'motion' and 'action'. Motion is the act of doing something that keeps you busy (planning, strategising, thinking about improvement). Whilst this is useful, these tasks will never produce an outcome by themselves. On the other hand, action is the act of working on something that will render a tangible result. This distinction between motion and action is pivotal, especially in educational settings. While motion can be seen as the groundwork, laying out theories and concepts, it is action that translates these ideas into practice, leading to impactful classroom practice. The summaries in *Teaching One-Pagers* are designed to be more than just a resource for motion; they are intended to instil action and serve as a catalyst for meaningful change. I hope you find them as useful as I have to drive self-improvement and support others to get better

In true fashion, the next double page is a one-pager summarising the one-pager concept (very meta). Following this, you will find the reader's guide which outlines the best way teachers can utilise and navigate this book.

JAMIE CLARK

Consider this book to be a 'starting point' if you're a teacher perhaps not au fait with cognitive science, or a refresher if you're a teacher who is more well-read.

JAMES CLEAR

When you're in motion, you're planning and strategising and learning. Those are all good things, but they don't produce a result. Action, on the other hand, is the type of behaviour that will deliver an outcome. (2018)

The One-Pager

The 'what', 'how' and 'why' of one-page summaries

JAMIE CLARK

One-pagers are summaries that add clarity to strategies, encourage deeper reading and inspire teachers to take action.

What are one-pagers and why are they useful?

This wouldn't be a book about one-pagers without a one-pager on one-pagers! Here's a summary of why this format is perfect for educators who want to boost their practice. Ultimately, one-pagers make professional development more manageable. They are intended to be sharp and to the point so that they can be read quickly, enabling teachers to take away valuable insights without investing too much of their non-contact time. The main advantages of one-pagers are that they are visually engaging, they communicate ideas with clarity, they serve as quick reference guides, they encourage reflection, and they promote collaboration. All this without the 'overwhelm' of a full book!

What a one-pager is and what it is not

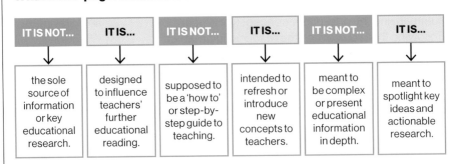

IT IS NOT...	IT IS...	IT IS NOT...	IT IS...	IT IS NOT...	IT IS...
the sole source of information or key educational research.	designed to influence teachers' further educational reading.	supposed to be a 'how to' or step-by-step guide to teaching.	intended to refresh or introduce new concepts to teachers.	meant to be complex or present educational information in depth.	meant to spotlight key ideas and actionable research.

Why are one-pagers an effective format?

One-pagers reduce cognitive load by presenting information in a concise, visually organised and easily digestible format. They leverage principles of design to make it easier for readers to absorb key information. Here are some of the main reasons why the one-pager format is effective:

CONCISENESS	VISUAL HIERARCHY	STORYTELLING AND FLOW	USE OF VISUALS
One-pagers...	One-pagers...	One-pagers...	One-pagers...
↓	↓	↓	↓
distil information to its essence and eliminate unnecessary details by presenting only the most crucial information.	structure content and guide readers' attention to the most important information using visual elements (headings, bullet points).	follow a logical flow or storytelling format to guide the reader through the information in a natural progression.	utilise white space and use graphs and diagrams to convey complex information more quickly and efficiently than text alone.

How can I use one-pagers for professional development?

PD NOTICEBOARDS

COACHING MEETINGS

PERSONAL COLLECTIONS

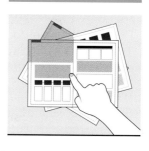

One-pagers are powerful staffroom conversation starters, helpful prompts to guide the direction of PD meetings (such as coaching feedback meetings) or even useful prompts for edu-book clubs. One-pagers are best used when they are printed off, pinned up, or presented on slide shows. Often summaries are interrelated and can be sequenced to form a progression of practical focus areas to form personalised 'playbooks' or to support professional learning workshops.

Reader's Guide

Teaching One-Pagers is a practical little book designed to refresh pedagogical knowledge, spark conversations and encourage deeper reading. Think of it a bit like a handbook that you can dip in and out of when you need a reminder or some educational inspiration. The content of the book has been organised into three main collections that cover three important areas relevant to most educational professionals:

Collection 1: Learning and Memory

A series of ideas and strategies surrounding the science of learning. These one-pagers address the main areas associated with Daniel Willingham's 'Simple Model of the Mind' and how learning happens.

Collection 2: Expert Teaching Principles

Six overarching principles that underpin day-to-day instructional teaching practices. Some of the practical strategies presented in this collection are explored in greater depth throughout the book.

Collection 3: Classroom Culture

Practical strategies focused on fostering a positive classroom culture. The summaries in this collection focus on developing high behavioural expectations and establishing good habits for learning.

Read More

Studies, books and blogs that are referenced throughout the one-pagers and inspired and influenced these collections.

For the best experience, I would suggest reading the book in order. However, if you're using it with colleagues or to support professional development, think of it as a pick-and-mix experience and browse the summaries that seem appropriate to you, so that you can tailor the ideas to your own school context. On social media, I have been delighted to see my posters pinned up next to professional learning bookshelves and displayed on noticeboards. This book is intended to be an equally practical resource to add to your professional learning library and I am excited to see how you use them in your school.

Despite organising the summaries into logical sections, not all ideas presented in this book can be neatly packaged into specific domains. For example, 'Cold Calling' does not only adhere to 'Cognitive Engagement' but it can be applied as an effective accountability strategy and therefore fits into the 'Secure Attention' section as well! In Collection 1, I have organised these overlaps into handy tables so you can easily see the crossovers.

The summaries also stick to a simple format: the 'what?', the 'why?' and the 'how?'. This structure serves as a clear road map to help you check your knowledge and implement relevant strategies accordingly. Here's a visual breakdown of what is included in each summary:

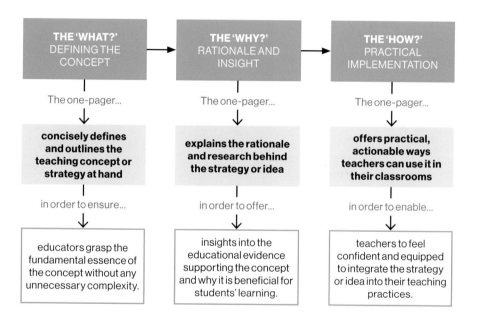

One-pagers are purposefully concise and provide a great starting point to build new knowledge. But, if you're an edu-fanatic like me, the 'Read More' suggestions at the bottom of each one-pager will be really helpful. Here you can find suggested books, blogs and research papers (even podcasts) that encourage deeper learning to boost your understanding beyond these pages. So, without further ado, let's begin with our first collection.

Learning and Memory:
A collection of one-pagers
summarising strategies
supporting the science of
learning and memory.

Learning and Memory

Explaining how learning happens using Daniel Willingham's Simple Model of the Mind

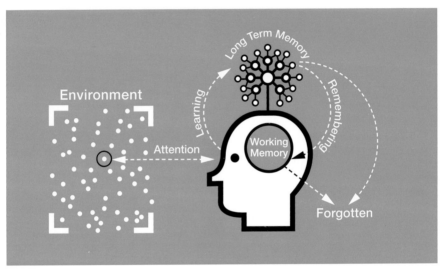

Daniel Willingham's 'Simple Model of the Mind' as interpreted by Oliver Caviglioli (image reproduced and manipulated with kind permission from @olicav)

As an experienced teacher, I have grown to recognise the importance of being 'evidence-informed'. For me, this isn't just a buzzword, it is a fundamental necessity for effective teaching. Over the years, my personal interest in cognitive science (and its application in the classroom) has helped me to refine my teaching toolkit and weed out ineffective techniques. I have replaced my somewhat naive approaches with a laser-focus on strategies that support memory and learning. I didn't learn this stuff as a graduate teacher. In fact, I hadn't a clue about how learning happened. In my mind, if a lesson was 'good' (resulting in reasonably engaged students and lots of written work) then students would 'learn something' by default. Now, I know this is not the case.

I think the best and most practical model to illustrate the learning process is Daniel Willingham's 'Simple Model of the Mind'. This diagram visualises how learning happens (and indirectly explains why it sometimes does not) in terms that even I can understand! This graphic has been extremely helpful for me when working with teachers who are puzzled as to why their 'great' lesson didn't seem to result in any actual learning.

Essentially, the diagram explains that working memory (your consciousness) holds the current thoughts and awareness of your surroundings ('I can smell my wife's delicious cooking', 'I can see my cat stretched out in the sunlight'). Like a huge filing cabinet, long-term memory stores networks of factual knowledge, residing outside of awareness until it is needed.

Learning occurs when there is a change in long-term memory and this change only happens when students actively *think*! Willingham famously asserts this idea in his memorable line, 'Memory is the residue of thought' (2010). Subsequently, the action of thinking leads to the strengthening of neural pathways in the brain, which in turn leads to the transfer and storage of knowledge in long-term memory. *Voilà*, learning and memory in a nutshell!

Of course, there is more to it than that. For example, it is also important to understand the role of the environment and maintaining cognitive attention, as well as the crucial aspect of schema building, remembering and cognitive load.

Taking inspiration from Tom Sherrington and Oliver Caviglioli's excellent *Teaching WalkThrus* series, I have dissected Willingham's model into five key areas which form the backbone of this collection (Secure Attention, Working Memory, Building Knowledge, Cognitive Engagement and Generative Processes).

The following one-pagers in **Collection 1: Learning and Memory** aim to address each area of the diagram and provide strategies that navigate around the fundamental cognitive problems it presents. While

DANIEL WILLINGHAM

People are naturally curious, but we are not naturally good thinkers; unless the cognitive conditions are right, we will avoid thinking. The implication of this principle is that teachers should reconsider how they encourage their students to think. (2010)

TOM SHERRINGTON

One of the most powerful ideas I've engaged with recently is using a diagram to visualise a shared model of the learning process. (2010)

these summaries don't claim to be exhaustive, they serve as a starting point for teachers like you who are looking to enhance their teaching practices with evidence-informed ideas.

So, before we delve into the summaries, let's take a minute to get a feel for the five key areas in this collection:

Secure Attention

Learning is closely tied to our focused attention. A lack of focus on relevant information can affect concentration and memory retention. The one-pagers under this heading focus on stripping out classroom distractions and offer strategies that enhance cognitive focus.

Working Memory

Our working memory is finite. In the classroom, this limitation means that teachers should use simple strategies to work around this constant by making new information more manageable. The summaries in this section outline strategies that help to optimise cognitive load.

Building Knowledge

As they learn, students form mental webs (schemas) and organise interconnected pieces of knowledge into hierarchies. This section contains a series of summaries to help students integrate knowledge and build schema.

Cognitive Engagement

Unlike working memory, long-term memory can store an almost limitless volume of information. To facilitate the transition of knowledge into long-term memory, teachers must drive thinking and provide feedback to ensure that new information is accurate.

Generative Processes

The more students engage in self-generation, the more likely knowledge will transfer to long-term memory. The one-pagers in this section assist teachers in engaging students to actively retrieve their existing schemas and encourage exploration of their knowledge.

AN OVERVIEW OF ONE-PAGERS IN COLLECTION 1: LEARNING AND MEMORY

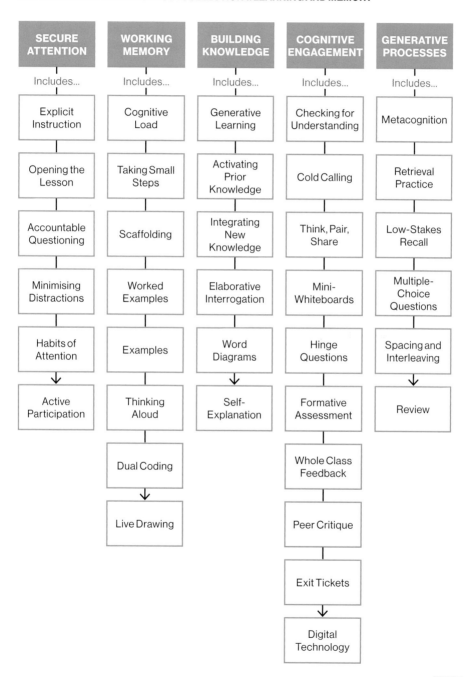

SECURE ATTENTION	WORKING MEMORY	BUILDING KNOWLEDGE	COGNITIVE ENGAGEMENT	GENERATIVE PROCESSES
Includes...	Includes...	Includes...	Includes...	Includes...
Explicit Instruction	Cognitive Load	Generative Learning	Checking for Understanding	Metacognition
Opening the Lesson	Taking Small Steps	Activating Prior Knowledge	Cold Calling	Retrieval Practice
Accountable Questioning	Scaffolding	Integrating New Knowledge	Think, Pair, Share	Low-Stakes Recall
Minimising Distractions	Worked Examples	Elaborative Interrogation	Mini-Whiteboards	Multiple-Choice Questions
Habits of Attention	Examples	Word Diagrams	Hinge Questions	Spacing and Interleaving
Active Participation	Thinking Aloud	Self-Explanation	Formative Assessment	Review
	Dual Coding		Whole Class Feedback	
	Live Drawing		Peer Critique	
			Exit Tickets	
			Digital Technology	

Why Don't Students Like School?

A cognitive scientist answers questions about how the mind works and what it means for the classroom

DANIEL WILLINGHAM

People are naturally curious, but we are not naturally good thinkers; unless the cognitive conditions are right, we will avoid thinking. (2010)

What are Willingham's main ideas?

Before we dig into the one-pagers, it's worth visiting ideas from Daniel Willingham's book *Why Don't Students Like School?*, where he writes, 'Unless the cognitive conditions are right, we will avoid thinking'. Thinking only occurs when you combine information from the environment and long-term memory in new ways; this combining of information happens in your working memory. Working memory has limited space, which means thinking becomes increasingly difficult as it gets crowded. To ensure students experience the joy of problem-solving, we should look at our practice from a cognitive perspective. Willingham suggests teachers should promote challenging cognitive work by 'reviewing each lesson in terms of what the student is likely to think about'.

Background knowledge: Willingham stresses the importance of background knowledge: 'Background knowledge from our long-term memory helps us to make sense of new information'. The factual knowledge stored in our long-term memory allows chunking, which increases space in working memory and makes it easier to tie ideas together. A practical way to do this is to get students to learn the concepts that come up again and again – the unifying ideas of each discipline. Knowledge is best learned when it is conceptual and facts are interrelated.

Memory: Students remember what they think about. Information cannot get into long-term memory unless it has first been in working memory. In other words, if you don't pay attention to something, you can't learn it: 'Memory is the residue of thought' (Willingham 2010). Thinking about meaning helps memory, and so teachers must design assignments so that students think about the meaning of content.

Understanding: We understand things we don't know by relating them to prior knowledge. This is why analogies work effectively when teaching students a new concept as they provide concrete examples. Willingham (2010) says, 'Understanding is disguised remembering because every new idea we have is built on existing ideas.' Our understanding of new information is initially shallow knowledge. To develop deep knowledge, we must work with the same idea in a number of ways, which can take time.

Practising: To increase competency and improve, we must practise. Willingham (2010) says that it's impossible to become proficient at a mental task without extended practice. Practice can make the mental process automatic and so requires little working memory capacity. This helps to extend thinking as more space in working memory can be used to further learning. Spacing practice over time is also useful as it leads to long-lasting memory. Practising lots of problems of a particular type makes it likely you will recognise the underlying structure of the problem.

Experts and novices: Experts are better equipped than novices to identify details and transfer knowledge more quickly to similar situations. Willingham explains that information in an expert's long-term memory is organised differently, as they can see the deep structures of concepts much more easily. Expert intuition is not a magical ability; it is a product of pattern recognition and mental schemas developed through years of practice and background knowledge.

Secure Attention	Working Memory	Building Knowledge	Cognitive Engagement	Generative Processes

Secure Attention

Strip out distractions and build habits that enhance cognitive attention in the classroom

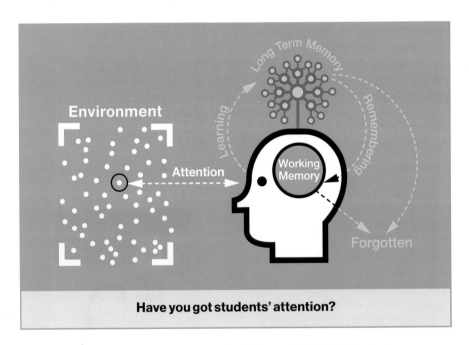

Have you got students' attention?

Students remember what they attend to (Mccrea 2017). If all students are paying attention to your explanations and thinking about the new information you are explaining, there is a greater chance learning will take place. However, like adults, students' minds can veer off down the road to distraction. Instead of focusing on what they're learning, students might divert their attention to extraneous matters. They may be thinking about passing a note to a mate or swinging on their chair, or they may even get distracted by the classroom display behind you.

DANIEL WILLINGHAM

Having the knowledge, tools and routines to quickly gain students' attention is fundamental to keeping students cognitively engaged. The following one-pagers summarise pedagogical approaches and chalk-face strategies that prioritise making students accountable so that they are all expected to think and participate in lessons. The suggested ideas presented for managing and securing attention focus on the following:

Although we like to think that we decide what to pay attention to, our minds have their own wishes and desires when it comes to the focus of attention. (2010)

- **Reducing learning environment distractions.**

- **Optimising teacher instruction and task design.**

- **Establishing attentional routines.**

Secure attention overlaps

The one-pagers in this section overlap with others and can arguably be applied to other aspects of Willingham's Simple Model of the Mind.

	Working Memory	Building Knowledge	Cognitive Engagement	Generative Processes
Explicit Instruction	✓		✓	
Opening the Lesson			✓	✓
Accountable Questioning	✓		✓	✓
Minimise Distractions	✓		✓	
Habits of Attention	✓		✓	
Active Participation			✓	

Secure Attention

Explicit Instruction

Make teaching direct, engaging and success focused

What is it and why is it effective?

Explicit instruction is a structured approach that provides clear instruction, design and delivery procedures to maximise learning. The approach is particularly effective for securing and maintaining students' attention. It focuses on active participation, which means holding students accountable by asking them to write, speak, or do something in response to the teacher's instruction. Explicit teaching also promotes the use of scaffolds to guide students through the learning process with clear explanations and supported practice. The goal of explicit instructional practices is to foster independence and mastery by regularly checking for understanding and ensuring successful participation by all students. Research shows that in order to reach proficiency and build fluency, both practise and specific feedback on the quality of students' work are key.

PAUL KIRSCHNER

The aim of all instruction is to alter long-term memory. If nothing has changed in LTM, nothing has been learned. (et al 2006)

What are the principles of explicit instruction?

Maximise student and engagement and learning by:

- optimising time on task and active participation.

- promoting high levels of success (80% accuracy).

- increasing content coverage to maximise learning.

- getting students to spend time in instructional groups.

- scaffolding instruction through providing support.

- addressing different forms of knowledge.

Read More: 'Why Minimal Guidance During Instruction Does Not Work' by Kirschner et al (2006)

How do I implement it?

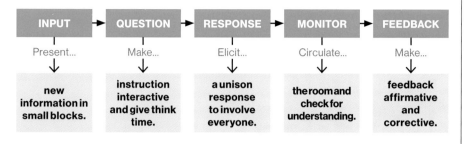

INPUT	QUESTION	RESPONSE	MONITOR	FEEDBACK
Present...	Make...	Elicit...	Circulate...	Make...
↓	↓	↓	↓	↓
new information in small blocks.	instruction interactive and give think time.	a unison response to involve everyone.	the room and check for understanding.	feedback affirmative and corrective.

Use the four key delivery skills

1 Require frequent responses from everyone.

2 Monitor student performance carefully.

3 Immediate affirmative and corrective feedback.

4 Deliver the explicit lesson at a brisk and lively pace.

Build fluency through practice:

Begin and conclude each lesson with a comprehensive review of the main skills or knowledge. During the main body of lessons, focus on modelling the concept or skill, and subsequently embed guided and independent practice sessions to build fluency. Aim for students to achieve high levels of success (80% correct/accurate).

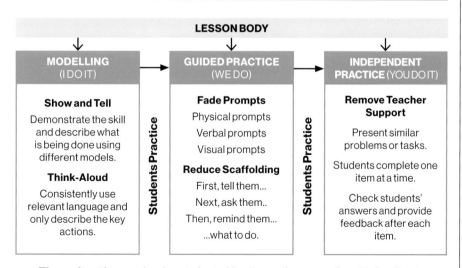

LESSON BODY

MODELLING (I DO IT)		GUIDED PRACTICE (WE DO)		INDEPENDENT PRACTICE (YOU DO IT)
Show and Tell Demonstrate the skill and describe what is being done using different models. **Think-Aloud** Consistently use relevant language and only describe the key actions.	Students Practice	**Fade Prompts** Physical prompts Verbal prompts Visual prompts **Reduce Scaffolding** First, tell them... Next, ask them.. Then, remind them... ...what to do.	Students Practice	**Remove Teacher Support** Present similar problems or tasks. Students complete one item at a time. Check students' answers and provide feedback after each item.

Throughout lesson: Involve students. Monitor performance. Provide feedback.

Secure Attention

Opening the Lesson

Set a clear focus and purpose from the beginning

What is it and why is it important?

Opening the lesson with purpose helps to establish a focused learning environment. Securing students' attention with well-planned introduction activities is a powerful way of activating students' prior knowledge so they are primed to learn and connect new ideas. Introducing retrieval practice activities can help to identify gaps in knowledge and strengthen existing schemas so that teachers can adapt and respond to students' needs in real time. Furthermore, this approach fosters a dynamic classroom culture where students are more engaged and motivated to actively participate.

How do I implement this?

Start with a 'Do Now' activity: A 'Do Now' is the name given to a short, low-stakes activity that students complete independently as soon as they enter the classroom. The aim of a 'Do Now' is to settle the class and activate prior knowledge by engaging students in low-stakes retrieval quizzes or short written responses. 'Do Now' activities can also be used to review retrieval homework questions and serve to gather information about student knowledge and progress over time. To work effectively, 'Do Now' activities must be embedded as a routine.

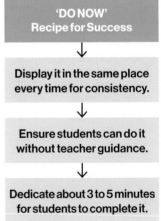

'DO NOW'
Recipe for Success

↓

Display it in the same place every time for consistency.

↓

Ensure students can do it without teacher guidance.

↓

Dedicate about 3 to 5 minutes for students to complete it.

Read More: How To Use Retrieval Practice To Improve Learning, retrievalpractice.org/library

Review prior knowledge: Introduce regular reviews into lesson starter routines to allow students to revisit prior knowledge and make connections between new information and information they already know. To help students to activate prior knowledge or to build requisite knowledge teachers can: generate class discussion, ask a range of questions, use visuals or media, and utilise resources like KWL charts ('What I Know', 'What I Want to Know', 'What I've Learned').

K 'The heart is a vital organ in the body.'

W 'What is the role of a valve in the heart?'

L 'The heart has four chambers.'

Most of you misunderstood...

Address errors or misconceptions: Start lessons by presenting students with a common misconception based on a previous topic they have studied, or from recent feedback. For example, this could be an incorrect problem or a poorly written paragraph that requires fixing. Build in time for students to correct the misconception independently (or with others) before reviewing it as a class.

Use low-stakes retrieval practice starters: Develop a range of effective retrieval practice strategies to draw upon. These strategies should reinforce students' schemas in different ways and allow them to deepen their understanding. It's beneficial for students to be familiar with the routines associated with each strategy. Each strategy should be cumulative, so they gradually increase in difficulty.

POOJA AGARWAL

We typically focus on getting information into students' heads, instead we need to focus on getting information out of students' heads.

1	Low-stakes quizzes

4	Free Recall

2	Concept Mapping

5	Flashcards

3	Summarising Ideas

6	Retrieval Boards

Secure Attention

Accountable Questioning

Boost thinking and participation from everyone

PRITESH RAICHURA

Every question the teacher asks interrupts the loss of attention. Questions are engaging; even more so when everyone is expected to show they are participating by putting their hand up. (2023a)

What is it and why is it important?

For effective learning, it is crucial for teachers to not only capture but also sustain students' focus on key aspects of the lesson. The only time you are learning is when your mind is thinking about the information you are learning. Accountable questioning plays a big role in this process. It is a strategy where every student is expected to be an active participant, ready to respond to questions posed by the teacher at any time. This method effectively secures attention, as students understand they could be called upon to offer their thoughts or understanding of the material at any moment during the class. More techniques of this ilk are explored further in Collection 1. For now, here are some powerful strategies that build attention and inspire motivation from sustained success.

How do I implement it?

Build classroom culture: For accountable questioning to thrive, schools must invest time making this approach the norm in the classroom.

OK, 3, 2, 1, all hands up!

Turn and talk to your partner. Go!

Read More: 'Checks for Listening: 100% Participation' by Pritesh Raichura

Embed 'No Opt Out': Doug Lemov in his book *Teach Like a Champion* (2010), describes this technique as a powerful method for ensuring consistent engagement and accountability. When a student is unable to answer a question, do not simply excuse them from the task. Instead, provide the answer or solicit it from another student and then return to the original student, asking them to repeat the correct response. This reinforces the expectation that every student must engage in the learning process.

Probe using a range of question types: Varying the use of question types helps to deepen students' thinking and probe their understanding.

CLARIFYING CONCEPTS	CHALLENGING BELIEFS	EXAMINING EVIDENCE
'What do we mean when we say "democracy"?' or 'Can you give me an example of that?'	'Why do you think that is true?' or 'What assumptions are we making about this issue?'	'What evidence do you have to support your view?' or 'How can we back up this argument?'

OTHER PERSPECTIVES	PROBING IMPLICATIONS	QUESTION THE QUESTION
'What might someone who disagrees with you say?' or 'How might this look from another perspective?'	'What are the consequences of this action?' or 'How would your answer affect this situation?'	'Why do you think this question is important?' or 'What do you think this question assumes?'

Employ 'Turn and Talk' strategy: Similar to the 'Think, Pair, Share' strategy, students are partnered up and prompted to discuss their thoughts or answers with each other following a teacher's question. This technique not only enables students to articulate and refine their ideas through peer interaction but also significantly boosts classroom engagement. This strategy is beneficial for students who might feel hesitant to speak up in a larger group.

Utilise 'All Hands Up Cold Calling': Teacher and school leader Pritesh Raichura advocates for what he calls 'all hands up cold calling'. This method diverges from traditional cold calling techniques by having all students raise their hands after a question is asked, regardless of whether they know the answer. This creates an energetic and participatory atmosphere, fostering a culture where every student is paying attention, visibly ready and eager to contribute.

Secure Attention

Minimising Distractions

Maintain students' mental attention

What is it and why is it important?

Distractions limit students' attentional bandwidth, that can otherwise be focused on learning. As educator and author Peps Mccrea (2020a) explains, attention is the 'gatekeeper to thinking'. Without thought, students will not learn – this is famously emphasised by Daniel Willingham: 'Memory is the residue of thought'. If students' working memory is clogged by extraneous sources of load, they will have less attention available for learning. Engaging students in cognitive work and minimising social, environmental and instructional distractions is imperative to the learning process.

PEPS MCCREA

*What we attend to
is what we learn.*
(2017)

How do I implement it?

Manage attention with questioning: Maintaining students' mental attention is important in engaging students in cognitive work. Purposeful questioning with accountability can assist in keeping student focused on the learning at hand because there is an expectation that they have to generate a response if called upon. Strategies such as Cold Calling and Think, Pair, Share are simple yet powerful methods to secure attention and enforce accountability.

Read More: Evidence Snacks by Peps Mccrea: 'Eliminate Potential Distractions'

FREE UP STUDENTS' ATTENTIONAL BANDWIDTH (MCCREA 2023)

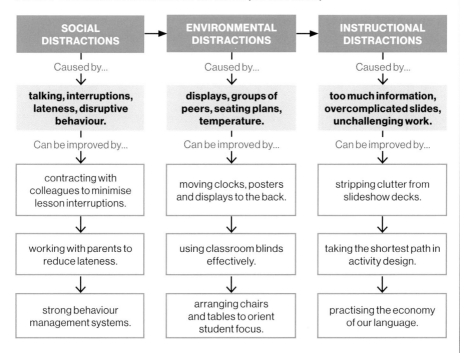

SOCIAL DISTRACTIONS	ENVIRONMENTAL DISTRACTIONS	INSTRUCTIONAL DISTRACTIONS
Caused by...	Caused by...	Caused by...
talking, interruptions, lateness, disruptive behaviour.	**displays, groups of peers, seating plans, temperature.**	**too much information, overcomplicated slides, unchallenging work.**
Can be improved by...	Can be improved by...	Can be improved by...
contracting with colleagues to minimise lesson interruptions.	moving clocks, posters and displays to the back.	stripping clutter from slideshow decks.
working with parents to reduce lateness.	using classroom blinds effectively.	taking the shortest path in activity design.
strong behaviour management systems.	arranging chairs and tables to orient student focus.	practising the economy of our language.

Direct students' attention: Use instructional methods to direct students' attention to important information. For example, use slides with reminders of prior learning and pause videos to direct attention, make instructions or checklists to maintain students' focus on important information only.

Simple lesson design: Avoid starting with what activities you want students to do. In the long run, this can become an exercise in keeping students busy. Instead, ask yourself 'What do I want my students to learn?' and design activities with a direct route to learning. This will assist in preventing unnecessary distractions.

Keep it silent: It is tempting to speak or give instructions after setting students an independent problem or task. The reality is that this distracts them from thinking.

Secure Attention

Habits of Attention

Build attentional habits using Doug Lemov's 'STAR' routine

What is it and why is it effective?

Habits of attention are routines that help students build strong attentional habits, particularly in eye-tracking and body language. 'STAR' (originally named 'SLANT') is an acronym created by Doug Lemov designed to teach students the behaviours and routines to develop a more inclusive learning environment where every students voice is heard and validated. Lemov (2020) stresses that the subtle cues that make up 'STAR' are established to communicate 'support for, and the belonging of speakers'. 'STAR' helps to build good habits for learning such as paying attention, actively listening to peers and active participation. Ultimately, *where* students look shapes their attention and therefore impacts whether they learn or not.

How do I implement it?

Reinforce routines:
Strategies such as 'STAR' only work if they become established as habits. This means encoding the process into the DNA of each lesson so that they happen naturally day in, day out. This can be achieved by consistently reinforcing the routine through reminders, narrating when it happens and projecting warmth.

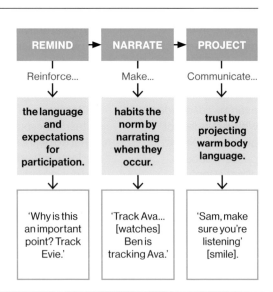

REMIND	NARRATE	PROJECT
Reinforce...	Make...	Communicate...
↓	↓	↓
the language and expectations for participation.	habits the norm by narrating when they occur.	trust by projecting warm body language.
↓	↓	↓
'Why is this an important point? Track Evie.'	'Track Ava... [watches] Ben is tracking Ava.'	'Sam, make sure you're listening' [smile].

Read More: *Teach Like a Champion 3.0* by Doug Lemov

What is 'STAR' and how do I implement it?

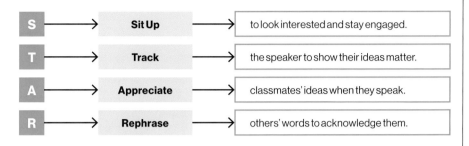

S	Sit Up	to look interested and stay engaged.
T	Track	the speaker to show their ideas matter.
A	Appreciate	classmates' ideas when they speak.
R	Rephrase	others' words to acknowledge them.

Sit up: When students are slouching or leaning back in their chairs, their body language is not primed for learning. Good posture can help students stay alert and focused during class. It is essential to teach students how to sit in the optimal position for learning: straight, with their backs against the seat, feet placed on the ground and hands on the desk (or arms crossed).

Track the speaker: Following the movements and gestures of the speaker is a visual cue to remain attentive. Tracking the speaker involves maintaining eye contact, observing body language, and paying attention to any visual aids or cues that are being used. By doing so, students visibly acknowledge the speaker, validate their ideas and show that they matter.

Appreciate: This component focuses on helping students to actively listen and appreciate their classmates' ideas and perspectives. Teach students that nodding is an effective non-verbal method to show agreement or understanding. Promote positive body language, such as smiling and maintaining eye contact when a classmate is speaking.

Rephrase: Encourage students to get into the habit of rephrasing the words of the previous person to show they were listening. This helps them to acknowledge the person's response but also allows them to offer their own ideas. Scaffold this with students by using verbal prompts: 'I agree with Mark's main point when he said...', 'I'd like to add...'.

DOUG LEMOV

The ability to sustain focus and concentration is the unacknowledged source of many students' success, and the inability to attend is the undoing of others. (2020)

Secure Attention

Active Participation

Elicit frequent responses from all students

What is it and why is it effective?

Active participation involves engaging all students to elicit responses that require them to speak, write, or perform actions. In her book *Explicit Instruction*, Dr. Anita Archer (2010) writes, 'In the act of [interactively] responding, students are retrieving, rehearsing, and practicing the information, concepts, skills, or strategies being taught'. Strategies that encourage regular physical, written and oral interaction not only allow the teacher to easily check for understanding but also help to secure students' attention and cultivate a learning environment where their involvement is expected.

ANITA ARCHER

Instructional lessons that are interactive make learning visible so teachers can ensure students are learning. (2010)

How do I implement it?

Make instruction interactive: Dr. Archer (2010) explains that for it 'to be truly effective, instruction must be interactive'. Frequent student participation helps to secure attention and improve learning. When eliciting frequent responses, a teacher presents a small amount of information and stops to ask for a response. The process follows a repeated cycle of 'input', 'question' and 'response'. Students are more likely to be engaged and on task when the lesson is delivered at a lively and brisk pace, which involves tight questioning and punchy feedback.

Read More: *Explicit Instruction* by Anita Archer and Charles A. Hughes

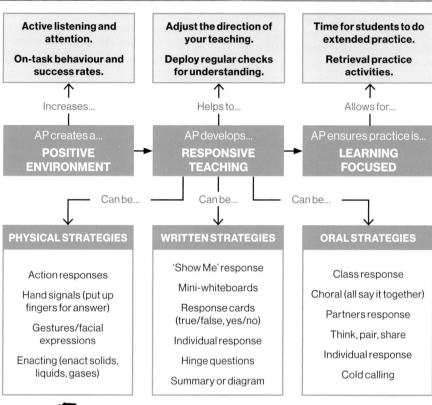

Active listening and attention. On-task behaviour and success rates.	Adjust the direction of your teaching. Deploy regular checks for understanding.	Time for students to do extended practice. Retrieval practice activities.
↑ Increases...	↑ Helps to...	↑ Allows for...
AP creates a... **POSITIVE ENVIRONMENT**	AP develops... **RESPONSIVE TEACHING**	AP ensures practice is... **LEARNING FOCUSED**

Can be... — Can be... — Can be...

PHYSICAL STRATEGIES	WRITTEN STRATEGIES	ORAL STRATEGIES
Action responses	'Show Me' response	Class response
Hand signals (put up fingers for answer)	Mini-whiteboards	Choral (all say it together)
Gestures/facial expressions	Response cards (true/false, yes/no)	Partners response
Enacting (enact solids, liquids, gases)	Individual response	Think, pair, share
	Hinge questions	Individual response
	Summary or diagram	Cold calling

Action responses:
Action responses involve physical movements such as hand signals, pointing (at features of a diagram) and enacting. Action responses are a more creative way to find out what students know.

Written responses:
Individual written responses support responsive teaching. For example, 'Show me boards' responses using mini-whiteboards allow the teacher to collect more data to inform the direction of their teaching.

Oral responses:
Invite individuals, partners, or the entire class to provide oral feedback. Unison responding involves participation from all students, whether in spoken or written form, in response to a familiar cue given by a teacher.

Secure Attention	**Working Memory**	Building Knowledge	Cognitive Engagement	Generative Processes

Working Memory

Managing and optimising students' cognitive load

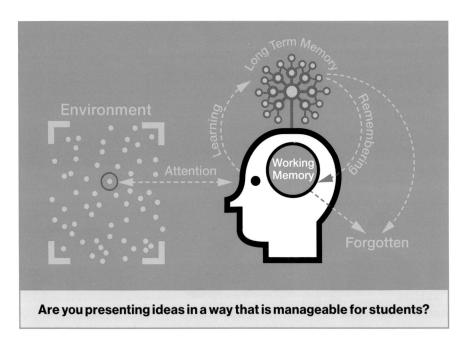

Are you presenting ideas in a way that is manageable for students?

Working memory is the part of our brain that holds and processes information in the short-term. Sweller's 'cognitive load theory' (1988) suggests that students' working memory is limited and only able to hold small chunks of information at a time (approximately seven items). This means teachers have to be mindful not to cognitively overload students' working memory by ensuring information is presented a structured and manageable way. Strategies such as sequencing information in small steps and implementing worked examples support students to manage information. We can also reduce extraneous cognitive load by using visual representations such as diagrams to capture transient information. Essentially, students learn more effectively when teachers plan with cognitive load in mind. The one-pagers in this section summarise strategies that support in addressing the limitations of working memory. They include:w

DYLAN WILIAM

I've come to the conclusion that Sweller's cognitive load theory is the single most important thing for teachers to know. (2017b)

- **Removing redundant information.**

- **Breaking information into manageable steps.**

- **Supporting the processing of new information.**

- **Utilising visual and verbal cognitive channels.**

Working memory overlaps

The one-pagers in this section overlap with others and can arguably be applied to other aspects of Willingham's Simple Model of the Mind.

	Securing Attention	Building Knowledge	Cognitive Engagement	Generative Processes
Cognitive Load	✓		✓	
Taking Small Steps		✓	✓	
Scaffolding			✓	
Examples		✓	✓	
Worked Examples	✓	✓	✓	
Thinking Aloud		✓	✓	
Dual Coding		✓	✓	✓
Live Drawing		✓	✓	✓

Working Memory

Cognitive Load

Tailor instruction to maximise learning outcomes

What is it and why is it important?

The cognitive load theory (CLT) emerged from the work of educational psychologist John Sweller in the 1980s and explores how cognitive load (or mental effort) required to process information impacts learning (Centre for Education Statistics and Evaluation 2017). To learn something new, knowledge must first be processed in working memory (WM) before being transferred and stored in long-term memory (LTM) in the form of 'schemas'. If WM is overloaded, there is a greater risk that the content being taught will not be understood by the learner. This knowledge of the human brain is critical for teachers because it helps them design teaching strategies that free up and optimise the load on students' working memories to help maximise learning.

OLLIE LOVELL

Intrinsic cognitive load is the load associated with the core learning taking place; it is the load that we want students' working memories to be occupied with. (2021)

What is intrinsic and extraneous cognitive load?

We must optimise intrinsic (good) cognitive load and reduce extraneous (bad) cognitive load.

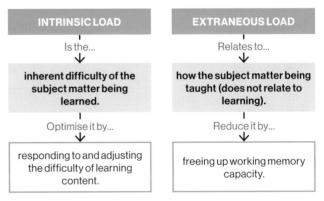

INTRINSIC LOAD	EXTRANEOUS LOAD
Is the...	Relates to...
inherent difficulty of the subject matter being learned.	how the subject matter being taught (does not relate to learning).
Optimise it by...	Reduce it by...
responding to and adjusting the difficulty of learning content.	freeing up working memory capacity.

Read More: *Sweller's Cognitive Load Theory in Action* by Ollie Lovell

How do I implement it?

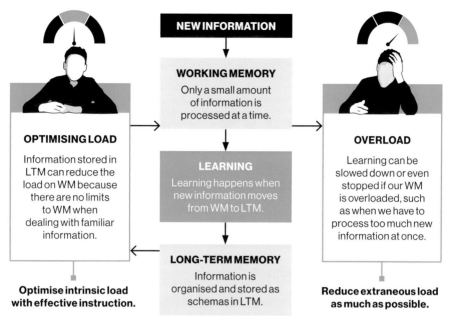

NEW INFORMATION

WORKING MEMORY
Only a small amount of information is processed at a time.

OPTIMISING LOAD

Information stored in LTM can reduce the load on WM because there are no limits to WM when dealing with familiar information.

LEARNING
Learning happens when new information moves from WM to LTM.

OVERLOAD

Learning can be slowed down or even stopped if our WM is overloaded, such as when we have to process too much new information at once.

Optimise intrinsic load with effective instruction.

LONG-TERM MEMORY
Information is organised and stored as schemas in LTM.

Reduce extraneous load as much as possible.

Increase independent problem solving: Fully guided instruction is effective for teaching new material, but as students become more skilled, it can become counterproductive. Excessive guidance can burden working memory. Faded worked examples that lead to independent problem-solving are more beneficial as students develop expertise over time.

Present essential information together: Cognitive overload can occur when students have to split their attention between two or more sources of information that are presented separately (know as the 'split attention effect'). This means teachers should design learning activities and resources with this information in mind, such as integrating labels into diagrams (not separating them in a list).

Cut out inessential information: Presenting students with inessential information can hinder learning and add extra load on their working memory (WM). To avoid this, cut out unnecessary details (known as the 'redundancy effect'). Also, consider chunking information into separate slides, removing irrelevant images, and providing spoken explanation only (referred to as the 'modality effect').

Working Memory

Taking Small Steps

Break down information to reduce cognitive load

What is it and why is it effective?

Teaching in small steps is a strategy that plays a crucial role in reducing the cognitive load on students' working memory, a concept emphasised in Rosenshine's 'Principles of Instruction' (2012), where it is suggested teachers should 'present new material in small steps with student practice after each step'. Given the limited capacity of working memory, it is vital to avoid overwhelming students with too much information at once, as this can lead to cognitive overload, making it easily forgotten. By breaking down information into manageable chunks, teachers not only facilitate better understanding but also gain insights into students' knowledge gaps, allowing for timely adjustments in teaching strategies. This approach not only makes learning more manageable but increases student motivation.

How do I implement it?

Find a good starting point: First, teachers should assess students' prerequisite knowledge to know where to build from. For example, when teaching punctuating direct speech, find out whether students know how speech marks are used. Organise the progression of skills that students need to know in a logical order and plan for dedicated practice opportunities at each stage of the learning journey.

Read More: 'Principles of Instruction' by Barak Rosenshine

Provide clear learning intentions: Well-written learning objectives provide a clear guide for learners about what they are expected to achieve at each step of the learning sequence. Make use of lists or checklists to help students see the skills or mark off the actions required at each step. For example, ask 'Have you… edited your work and checked for proper use of capital letters and full stops?'

BARAK ROSENSHINE

Present new material in small steps with student practice after each step: only present small amounts of new material at any time, and then assist students as they practice this material. (2012)

Practice to solidify new knowledge: When students first encounter new material, it is often hazy and not fully understood. To help students consolidate chunks of new knowledge, teachers can use mini-whiteboards to check for understanding and allow students to practice. This is effective because it is low-stakes and so students feel safer in making mistakes and, in turn, it is more likely to boost their confidence when tackling similar problems.

Break it up, model each step and allow for practice: Start by modelling a concept, skill, or part of a process. For example, a primary maths teacher might model how demonstrate how to define, apply and check the process of finding the area of a rectangle. Throughout this process, they might provide short practice opportunities to consolidate new learning.

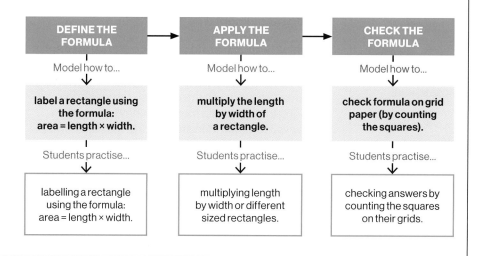

DEFINE THE FORMULA	APPLY THE FORMULA	CHECK THE FORMULA
Model how to…	Model how to…	Model how to…
label a rectangle using the formula: area = length × width.	multiply the length by width of a rectangle.	check formula on grid paper (by counting the squares).
Students practise…	Students practise…	Students practise…
labelling a rectangle using the formula: area = length × width.	multiplying length by width or different sized rectangles.	checking answers by counting the squares on their grids.

Working Memory

Scaffolding

Support students in developing independence

What is it and why is it important?

Scaffolding is a process where a temporary support is used to assist learners in gaining proficiency. The amount of scaffolding you use depends on the needs of each student in your class. As the metaphor suggests, scaffolds should always be deconstructed and eventually removed as students improve. Barak Rosenshine identified scaffolding as a key instructional procedure. As illustrated in the continuum opposite (originally created by Shaun Allison and Andy Tharby in *Making Every Lesson Count*), the process of scaffolding helps students move from being fully dependent on the teacher to being independent and fluent in applying skills to new contexts. Scaffolds and supports enable all students to establish clear starting points and fully engage in learning.

BARAK ROSENSHINE

Provide scaffolds for difficult tasks... scaffolds are gradually withdrawn as learners become more competent.
(2010)

How do I implement it?

Use visual supports and sentence starters: Graphic organisers, pictures and knowledge organisers can all help in scaffolding students' thinking and organising their ideas. Visual learning aids assist students in capturing transient information so they have more space available in working memory to think and grapple with new knowledge. Similarly, sentence starters or key vocabulary printed on resources or written on the whiteboard can offer a starting point for students, helping them to structure their thoughts and responses as they become more familiar with the material and engage in deeper learning.

Read More: *Rosenshine's Principles in Action* by Tom Sherrington

Use vocabulary checklists: Employ checklists of key vocabulary to support students when rehearsing and practising writing or verbalising key concepts. Checklists help break down the task into steps and allow students to self monitor their work. For example: 'Have I found...?', 'Did I use...?', 'Did I include...?', 'Does it link to...?'.

DEPENDENCE

Teacher explains and models new content. Students are listening and taking notes on key ideas.

Think aloud as you teach: Thinking aloud is an effective form of scaffolding. This strategy allows you to externalise your knowledge and provides novice learners with an opportunity to observe expert thinking. Use metacognitive language that makes your thinking transparent. For example, say things like, 'I'll summarise this part of...', 'So far...', 'Because of...', 'I predict...', 'I already know...', 'So this must be...', 'Next, I will...'.

HEAVY GUIDANCE

Teacher leads practice through regular questioning, discussion, scaffolding and lots of support.

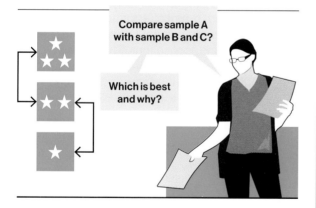

Compare sample A with sample B and C?

Which is best and why?

LIGHT GUIDANCE

Students are doing cognitive work on their own with regular teacher feedback and fewer supports.

INDEPENDENCE

Students work with new knowledge without teacher support. The cognitive work is passed on.

Show and compare exemplar work: Display and contrast examples of work of varying quality to show students exactly what success looks like. Dedicate time in class to collaborate with students to highlight and annotate key features in each exemplar so that they can use them as support throughout their practice. Gradually phase out these aids to empower students to develop self-confidence and self-sufficiency in their learning.

AUTONOMY

Students fluently manipulate knowledge and skills independently by applying them to new contexts.

Working Memory

Examples

Connect abstract ideas with real-world applications

What are they and why are they effective?

Using examples is a powerful method where teachers present specific ideas to illustrate a concept, principle, or process to students. For instance, in a history lesson, a teacher might use specific historical events to demonstrate the causes and effects of a particular war. This technique is highly effective when the examples are relevant, relatable and varied, as it offers students a concrete understanding of abstract ideas. In other words, examples help to form clear connections between content and real-world applications. They act as anchors in the learning process, enabling students to ask questions like, 'How does this example illustrate the rule?', 'What stays the same and what changes in each example?', or 'How does example A relate to example B?'.

How do I implement them?

Utilise concrete examples: To improve their explanations, teachers should provide concrete examples that help students visualise a broader concept so that new information is more tangible and understandable. For instance, in teaching the concept of gravity, a physics teacher might drop various objects to demonstrate how gravity affects them similarly, regardless of their size or shape. Concrete examples anchor abstract concepts in real-world applications that help students to see and grasp complex ideas.

See how gravity acts consistently on different objects?

Read More: *Educational Psychology: A Cognitive View* by David Ausubel

Refer to non-examples: Non-examples are when teachers present new information that does not fit a particular concept, aiding students to identify the concept's boundaries. For instance, when teaching about renewable energy sources, a teacher might discuss non-renewable sources like coal and oil to highlight and explain the main differences.

Go from general to specific: David Ausubel's 'subsumption theory' (1963) emphasises that the most general ideas of a subject should be presented first, followed by progressively differentiated details and specifics. This helps students to integrate new material with previously presented information. When presenting multiple examples, draw attention to the changing elements compared with the constant factors.

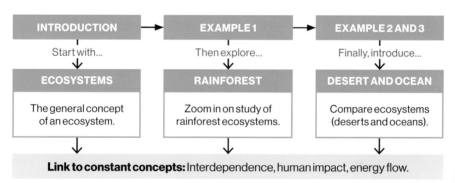

INTRODUCTION	EXAMPLE 1	EXAMPLE 2 AND 3
Start with...	Then explore...	Finally, introduce...
ECOSYSTEMS	RAINFOREST	DESERT AND OCEAN
The general concept of an ecosystem.	Zoom in on study of rainforest ecosystems.	Compare ecosystems (deserts and oceans).

Link to constant concepts: Interdependence, human impact, energy flow.

Display examples close together in time: By presenting examples in rapid sequence or simultaneously, enables students to hold multiple examples in their working memory at once. This makes it easier to compare and contrast these examples because it minimises the cognitive load of recalling each example from long-term memory. For example, in a history lesson about different forms of government, a teacher might present examples of democracy, monarchy and dictatorship side by side and leave this on the screen to support their explanation. Ask students to spot the difference and engage in think, pair, share to generate paired talk.

DAVID AUSUBEL

The most general ideas of a subject should be presented first and then progressively differentiated in terms of detail and specificity. (1963)

Working Memory

Worked Examples

Reduce cognitive load by demonstrating learning step-by-step

What are they and why are they effective?

A worked example is a step-by-step demonstration of how to solve a problem or task. It is a form of scaffolding that involves explanations of individual steps, the reasoning behind them and the results of the actions taken. Worked examples are useful when starting a new topic as they provide a bridge between teacher explanation and independent practice. By working through a series of worked examples, novice learners can see how an expert approaches and solves problems. Worked examples also reduce the cognitive load of students by breaking down complex processes into smaller, manageable steps. This frees up working memory so students can focus on the process and not just the answer.

JOHN SWELLER

Worked examples can efficiently provide us with the problem solving schemas that need to be stored in long-term memory. (et al 2011)

How do I implement them?

Utilise think-alouds: When creating worked examples, ask experienced teachers what common challenges students face with particular concepts. Use this information to inform your think-alouds and externalise your thoughts by explaining how to solve the problem. Afterwards, encourage students to self-explain the problem or explain it to a peer. This metacognitive strategy helps students to monitor their learning.

When approaching a problem like this, I usually start by...

Read More: 'Cognitive Load Theory: Research that Teachers Really Need to Understand' by CESE

Use visual aids to capture transient information: Use visual aids such as diagrams, graphs, or flowcharts to help clarify the steps of your worked examples and illustrate the problem-solving process. Dr. Fred Jones advocates the use of 'Visual Instruction Plans' (VIPs), which serve as a series of visual prompts that a student can refer to. VIPs work as a complete set of plans that show the step-by-step process. Like flat-pack furniture instructions, they often include visuals and minimal words for each step.

Employ completion tasks: Gradually increase the number of steps that students are required to complete until they can solve a full problem independently. Start by giving students a fully worked example as a reference point. Next, provide students with a similar problem that requires them to complete the final step. Partially completed models allow you to draw attention to specific parts of the process. Gradually fade your support over time so that students end up doing the work themselves.

Make deliberate mistakes: When students have sufficient prior knowledge, an effective idea is to incorporate worked examples that include hidden misconceptions and mistakes. This can stimulate discussion about why answers are incorrect and help students avoid making similar errors in their own work. Analysing why solutions are wrong helps to develop a deeper understanding.

Alternate between 'I do' and 'You do' practice: Worked examples are problems that you solve together with students before they apply their learning and commence independent practice. Alternating between the 'I do' phase and 'you do' phase, helps to break up information into manageable chunks. This strategy prevents overloading students' working memory.

Working Memory

Thinking Aloud

Reveal the thought process of an expert learner

What is it and why is it effective?

Thinking aloud is a form of modelling where teachers externalise their expert subject knowledge and skill to novice learners. For instance, while solving a problem, a mathematics teacher might articulate each step, providing a clear road map for students. This method is most effective when students actively participate in the activity and then practice it themselves. By adopting this approach, learners gradually develop a robust internal dialogue, learning to pose metacognitive questions such as, 'What is the task asking of me?', 'Which errors do I typically make?', or 'Where should I begin?'. Such internal scaffolding, cultivated over time, becomes a crucial tool to support students' future learning.

ALEX QUIGLEY

Revealing the thought processes of an expert learner helps to develop pupils' metacognitive skills. (2018)

TOPIC 3

⇕

TOPIC 2

⇕

TOPIC 1

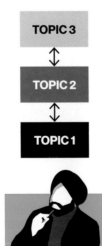

How do I implement it?

Make connections to prior learning: When thinking aloud, begin by addressing prerequisite background knowledge. Activating prior knowledge gives students a solid starting point and provides a platform on which to build new information. Teachers can facilitate this by asking questions such as: 'What do I know about problems like this?' and 'What ways of solving them have I used before?'.

Read More: 'Metacognition and Self-regulated Learning Guidance Report' by the EEF

Make explicit links and ask questions: As you progress through each step of a problem, engage in metacognitive talk by verbalising your decisions and methods. Make explicit links between each step to show their differences or how they relate. For example: 'In the last step, we looked at X...', 'Now, let's look at how to do Y...', 'Both parts are important because...'. Think-alouds require the teacher to speak slowly and invite active participation by asking questions such as: 'In this step, I need to use X... How did I do this last time?'

PREDICTING	VISUALISING	CONNECTING
Say things like...	Say things like...	Say things like...
↓	↓	↓
'Next, I predict...'	**'In my mind, I can see...'**	**'This problem is similar to...'**

Provide scaffolds to develop internal dialogue: After modelling, the aim is to develop students' metacognitive voice to elucidate what is happening below the surface. Support their development by providing appropriate scaffolds during practice sessions, such as giving students a list of sentence starters.

Invite participation: Make it clear that you are a learner too and you're capable of getting stuck or making errors. This will give you a chance to identify common misconceptions and reassure students. Verbalise the potential problems and pitfalls: 'I'm not sure how to do this, because...'. Crucially, you should verbalise how to approach specific problems and demonstrate how to fix them. Say things like: 'OK, the first thing I should do is...', 'I will start by...'. Over time, students will develop their own internal dialogue to deal with similar encounters in their learning.

$$\frac{3x + 2 = 12}{3x + 2 = 12}$$

'OK. Where am I now? Now I have $3x = 12$. I still need x by itself. I remember that I need to divide both sides. Why?'

↑

$$3x + 2 = 14$$
$$-2 = -2$$

'Look at this now. There is a 2 that I need remove. How do I do this? Can you help? Why should I subtract the 2?'

↑

$$3x + 2 = 14$$

'I am looking at this algebra problem and know I need x by itself. What have I done before in similar problems?'

↑

Working Memory

Dual Coding

Combine words with visuals to enhance learning

RICHARD E. MAYER

People learn more deeply from words and pictures than from words alone. (2005a)

What is it and why is it effective?

The dual coding theory states that we have two cognitive channels that help us encode information in long-term memory: a channel for processing words, such as written text and speech, and a channel for processing images, including shapes, sounds, or actions. Dual coding refers to the representation of information in long-term memory *after* instruction – if the memory trace includes both word-based and image-based components that have been interconnected then the key idea has been dual coded (Lovell 2021). To increase the likelihood of dual coding information in long-term memory, teachers can utilise the modality effect during instruction by presenting information in various ways, such as combining written or spoken words with graphics.

How does it link to cognition?

Given that our working memory is limited, activating both channels in tandem distributes the cognitive load and enables teachers to present more information without risking an overload of students' working memory.

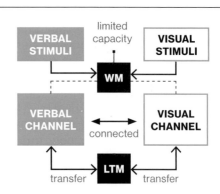

Read More: *Dual Coding with Teachers* by Oliver Caviglioli

How do I implement it?

Utilise dual modality instruction: When presenting new information, simultaneously show visuals and speak out loud, engaging the full capacity of students' verbal and visual working memory channels. Boost your graphics by using the following formats, combined with a spoken explanation (Clark 2009). To counteract the transient nature of spoken words, provide your notes in written form (such as a hand out) after the lesson.

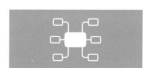

Representational: Use representational graphics to illustrate the object or content through life-like line drawings.

Mnemonic: Use these graphics to support the recall of facts and concepts by combining image and word cues.

Organisational: Use these graphics to represent qualitative relationships in charts, maps or tree diagrams.

Relational: Use relational graphics to show quantitative relationships in line graphs, pie charts and bar graphs.

Transformational: Use these graphics to show change in time or space through line drawings with movement arrows.

Interpretive: Use these graphics to build understanding of abstract content or processes using labelled images.

Employ graphic organisers: Graphic organisers help students to organise their schemas so that information is more likely to be encoded in long-term memory and subsequently retrieved. Implement tools like mind maps, flowcharts, Venn diagrams and concept maps. These organisers help students visually categorise, organise and link information.

Visualise information with diagrams: Diagrams break down complex ideas into simpler visual pieces, making it easier for students to understand and piece together various parts of a concept. When using diagrams, integrate words and draw attention to key parts with arrows.

Produce simple drawings with words: Drawing information encourages students to elaborate on their understanding and consider the information carefully to decipher how best to represent it. Simple representations of concepts and even linear timelines work effectively.

Working Memory

Live Drawing

Give illustrated representations using a visualiser

ROBERT MARZANO

Creating a nonlinguistic representation helps students deepen their understanding because it requires them to think about the content in new ways. (2010)

What is it and why is it effective?

A practical method of introducing dual coding with students is live drawing in class. This can be done by projecting example work to the board with visualiser or mirroring the screen of a tablet. Live drawing involves creating simple diagrams or illustrating a process in real time which the teacher then unpacks and explains step-by-step. This is followed by students actively replicating and rehearsing the teacher's example to consolidate learning. Live drawing combined with thinking aloud enables teachers to chunk information, externalise and explain expert knowledge step-by-step. It is useful in subjects that rely on non-linguistic representations such as science and geography.

How do I implement it?

Connect and display: Start by connecting a visualiser (or a similar projection device) displaying a blank page or mini-whiteboard to your class. Sit at the front of the class and face your students. Ensure that everyone can see the page from their seats before you start drawing.

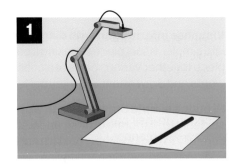

Read More: *Organise Ideas* by Oliver Caviglioli and David Goodwin

Draw and label: Begin to gradually draw the concept or new information. While drawing, explain each part of your illustration. When adding annotations or labels, remain silent so you have students' full attention, allowing them to read without distraction.

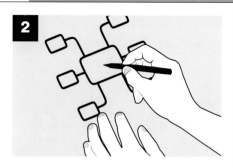

Pause and read: Enforce a period of silence giving students a few quiet moments to observe your drawing and read your labels or annotations. If needed, check for understanding. Once you believe they are ready, regain their attention before you proceed with the drawing.

Explain and point: While explaining, use your finger to trace the diagram or illustration, pointing to key parts. Direct students' attention by saying phrases such as, 'Look at the...' or, 'This part is important because...' Cold call to check for understanding before concluding.

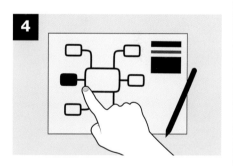

Recreate and rehearse: After completing the drawing, instruct students to copy it into their books. Subsequently, have them take turns explaining the concept or procedure to their partner in a step-by-step manner. Circulate the room to identify and address any misconceptions.

Secure Attention	Working Memory	**Building Knowledge**	Cognitive Engagement	Generative Processes

Building Knowledge

Integrating new knowledge and building schemas

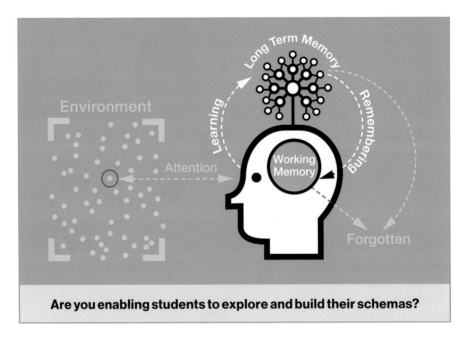

Are you enabling students to explore and build their schemas?

In cognitive science, building knowledge concerns the development of schema. Schemas are interconnected mental structures that represent our understanding of concepts. Teachers should provide opportunities for students to explore and build schema by recognising links between prior learning and the knowledge and skills learned in the current lesson. American psychologist, David Ausubel (1978) explains that this connection makes learning meaningful. He states: 'The most important single factor influencing learning is what the learner already knows.' Furthermore, chunking information to make it more digestible makes it easier for students to relate and assimilate new pieces of knowledge. This relates to Daniel Willingham's ideas in *Why Don't Students Like School?* (2010): 'understanding is disguised remembering' because every new idea we have is built on existing ideas. With this in mind, the one-pagers in this section summarise ideas that help with schema building and making meaning. They include how teachers can:

- **integrate new information into existing schema.**

- **warm up and activate prior knowledge.**

- **probe and solidify understanding.**

ARTHUR SHIMAMURA

Throughout the learning process it is critical to establish meaningful chunks of new information and relate them to existing knowledge. (2018)

Building knowledge overlaps

The one-pagers in this section overlap with others and can arguably be applied to other aspects of Willingham's Simple Model of the Mind.

	Secure Attention	Working Memory	Cognitive Engagement	Generative Processes
Generative Learning				✓
Activating Prior Knowledge		✓	✓	✓
Integrating New Knowledge		✓	✓	✓
Elaborative Interrogation		✓	✓	✓
Word Diagrams		✓		✓
Self and Peer Explanation			✓	✓

Building Knowledge

Generative Learning

Design tasks that help students construct meaning

What is it and why is it important?

Generative learning is the theory that learning occurs when we forge connections between new information and our background knowledge. Our brains do not just passively absorb the events or information in the environment but actively construct perceptions about our experiences. This frames learning as an active task that requires effort from learner to construct and develop knowledge. Throughout this process, our minds go through three stages to help us actively make sense of new information.

SELECTION	ORGANISATION	INTEGRATION
is the...	is when...	is when...
part of new information you pay attention to and process in WM.	the mind reorganises and gives context to new information.	the new information is linked to our prior knowledge in LTM.

Research indicates that new information is easily lost if it is not linked and integrated into existing knowledge. Generative learning influences the way teachers plan and implement activities for their students. In Fiorella and Mayer's research, they advocate the following eight simple strategies teachers can use to encourage students to make links between new information and prior knowledge. We will explore some of these strategies in more detail as we progress through the 'Building Knowledge' collection.

Read More: *Fiorella & Mayer's Generative Learning in Action* by Mark and Zoe Enser

How do I implement it?

Summarising: Teach students to summarise by choosing the most relevant information from the lesson and organising it into topics. Encourage them to use headings, subheadings and make links to their previous learning.

Mapping: Employ scaffolds such as graphic organisers to assist students in transforming newly acquired information into concept or knowledge maps. Model how to spatially arrange information with boxes and arrows.

Drawing: Demonstrate how to produce simple line drawings. Encourage students to visualise information by producing labelled graphics such as diagrams.

Imagining: Get students to create mental images to represent the main ideas from the lesson. Give prompts and model the process to facilitate their imagining.

LOGAN FIORELLA

Generative learning enable[s] learners to apply their knowledge to new situations. (2023)

Self-testing: Implement regular retrieval practice exercises to get students to recall prior learning. Effective methods include quizzing and free recall.

Self-explaining: Teach students to explain to themselves what they just learned using how and why questions. Provide questions that incorporate prior knowledge.

Teaching: Offer a structure and scaffolds to support students in teaching each other about a specific topic or concept. Challenge them to link ideas back to previous learning content.

Enacting: Select the most relevant information from a topic and act it out. Encourage students to use gestures, movement and facial expressions to bring ideas to life and make them more tangible.

Building Knowledge

Activate Prior Knowledge

Build bodies of connected knowledge

What is it and why is it important?

To achieve meaningful learning, teachers should activate students' prior knowledge so that they can more easily make connections between what they are learning and what they already know. Background knowledge serves as the foundation on which to build new schema. Before teaching new information, it's crucial to warm up the students and bring existing knowledge to mind. As Peps Mccrea explains (2023), readily available information is more likely to stick to new ideas: 'Prior knowledge is like 'glue for new ideas'. But it's more like a hot-melt glue for a glue gun than superglue... it's stickiest when warmed up.'

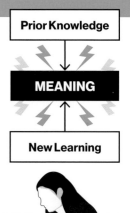

How do I make learning more meaningful (2023a):

1	Explicitly state the connections between new and existing knowledge.	**2**	Start by teaching the recurrent and general curriculum concepts and ideas.	**3**	Set tasks to help students make the connections (e.g. self-explanation).
4	Check for meaning carefully to ensure students have secure connections.	**5**	Get students to revisit and retrieve forgotten information.	**6**	Provide consistent meaningful learning opportunities over time.

Read More: *Ausubel's Meaningful Learning in Action* by Sarah Cottinghatt

How do I implement it?

Start broad and narrow it down: We tend to organise our schema hierarchically. This means teaching broader concepts first can aid students in connecting to new learning. For example, before reading the play, an English teacher might begin a unit on *Macbeth* by providing students with historical context about King James I and Elizabethan views on the supernatural. This broader body of information provides the glue to make new information about character and theme easier to grasp.

SARAH COTTINGHATT

We want students who have developed bodies of connected knowledge. (2023b)

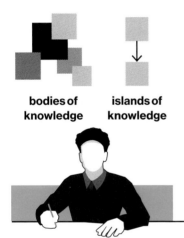

bodies of knowledge   **islands of knowledge**

Offer an organised overview of curriculum ideas: Author and educator, Sarah Cottinghatt (née Cottingham 2023b) explains that only bodies of knowledge will enable students to deeply understand ideas. So teachers should 'think bodies of knowledge not islands of knowledge'. Providing a visual overview of knowledge through tools like advance organisers is an effective method for illustrating the relationships between different ideas.

Make predictions: Encourage students to make predictions about new learning based on what they already know about a topic with similar underlying ideas. For example, drawing on their understanding of the conventions of Shakespearean tragedies, predict the fate of Macbeth at the end of the play.

DAVID AUSUBEL

The most important single factor influencing learning is what the learner already knows. (Cottingham 2023c)

Facilitate paired talk or self-explanation: Encouraging students to verbalise their understanding of a previous topic can help warm students up and activate their prior knowledge. Pose an open question and follow it with a think, pair, share routine or self-explanation activity.

Building Knowledge

Integrating New Knowledge

Relate new information to existing knowledge

What is it and why is it important?

Providing time for students to relate and integrate information is an important aspect of establishing a stable and coherent body of knowledge. Activities that support students with connecting knowledge helps to strengthen their initial connections and make new learning stick before they move on to building fluency through retrieval practice. In his paper 'MARGE: A Whole-Brain Learning Approach for Students and Teachers', neuroscientist Arthur Shimamura (2018) advises teachers to employ methods that 'engage the learner by relating and integrating new information as meaningful links to existing knowledge'.

GRAHAM NUTHALL

Students need several different interactions with relevant content for [it]... to be integrated into their long-term memory. (2007)

How does this link with multiple exposures?

Professor Graham Nuthall in his book *The Hidden Lives of Learners* (2007), explains that presenting the same material in different ways (and spacing this process out over time), aids in transferring new learning into the student's long-term memory. Providing diverse ways for students to engage with material helps them to develop deep knowledge as they become proficient in recognising the underlying structures of concepts. Revisiting specific topics in the curriculum through a spiraling approach is beneficial for ensuring multiple exposures.

Read More: *MARGE: A Whole-Brain Learning Approach for Students and Teachers* by Arthur Shimamura

How do I implement it?

Relate using the 3Cs: Arthur Shimamura's 3Cs approach can support students with integrating knowledge and organising their schemas.

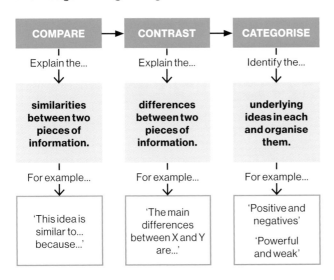

ARTHUR SHIMAMURA

The simple act of generating questions and providing answers helps to integrate new facts into your knowledge database. (2018)

Chunk information into manageable blocks: Break activities down so that students can engage in more manageable segments. For instance, ask guiding questions to steer students through a self or peer explanation task: 'Explain how light absorption functions in photosynthesis'. Students could also write a short paragraph to summarise each key aspect of a new concept or process.

Use mnemonics: Shimamura (2018) points out that 'sometimes we need to learn seemingly arbitrary associations that have no inherent meaningfulness'. It can be effective for students or teachers to create mnemonics or acronyms as exemplified in this approach for treatment for minor injuries.

R	**Rest** to prevent further damage.
I	**Ice** to control inflammation.
C	**Compression** to stop swelling.
E	**Elevation** to drain excess fluids.

Elaborative Interrogation

Ask 'how' and 'why' questions to deepen understanding

What is it and why is it effective?

Elaborative interrogation is a learning strategy in which students ask and answer 'why' and 'how' questions about the material they are studying. Rather than simply memorising facts, students explain the underlying reasons and connections between ideas, which helps create a bridge between students' new knowledge and their existing knowledge. Encouraging students to engage in deeper thinking about the material not only facilitates a greater understanding and knowledge acquisition on the topic but also serves as an effective tool for identifying knowledge gaps. This process bolsters long-term memory, aiding knowledge retention.

YANA WEINSTEIN

Elaborative interrogation encourages you to think about relationships between different ideas. (et al 2016)

How do I implement it?

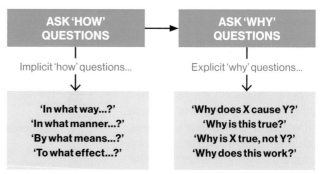

ASK 'HOW' QUESTIONS	ASK 'WHY' QUESTIONS
Implicit 'how' questions...	Explicit 'why' questions...
'In what way...?' 'In what manner...?' 'By what means...?' 'To what effect...?'	'Why does X cause Y?' 'Why is this true?' 'Why is X true, not Y?' 'Why does this work?'

Read More: The Learning Scientists website www.learningscientists.org

The Physics of Flight (Weinstein et al 2018)

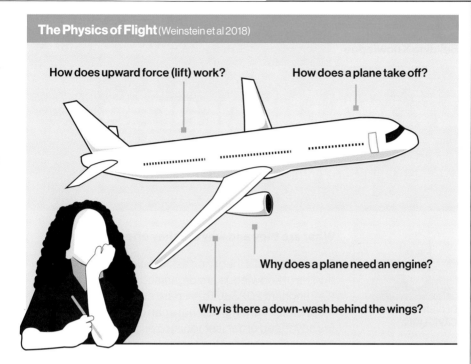

How does upward force (lift) work?

How does a plane take off?

Why does a plane need an engine?

Why is there a down-wash behind the wings?

Model precise elaborative interrogation questions: The more specific and detailed the elaborative interrogation questions are, the greater their impact. For example, when studying the physics of flight, instead of asking 'Why is there a down-wash?', ask 'Why is there a down-wash behind the wings?' Crafting detailed 'why' and 'how' questions requires modelling and practice. This might involve the teacher initially generating questions with the class during the early stages of the process.

Offer question starters for generating questions: Scaffold elaborative interrogation for students by providing generic question starters to initiate their thinking. For example: 'What are the strengths and weaknesses of...?' or 'Explain why ... is important'. Get students to work in pairs or individually to write as many questions as possible.

Encourage students to self-explain: After interrogating material with 'why' and 'how' questions, prompt students to produce their own explanations for these questions. This analytical approach moves students beyond recall of factual information and pushes them to into deeper thinking as they have to provide valid explanations.

Building Knowledge

Word Diagrams

Organise ideas into visual hierarchies and sequences

OLIVER CAVIGLIOLI

Without organisation, knowledge content is a mere list of discrete facts. But by organising them through forging connections creates meaning. (2021)

What are they and why are they effective?

David Ausubel's theory on assimilation explains that bodies of knowledge are organised hierarchically (Cottingham 2023c). To prepare students for meaningful learning, teachers can use word diagrams (as advanced organiser tools) to order information and cognitively prepare students to learn new material. Word diagrams are word-only graphic organisers that categorise information and help students to see ideas as objects. In *Organise Ideas*, Caviglioli and Goodwin (2021) explain how word diagrams consist of containers (to cluster information) or paths (to order information). Additionally, word diagrams are an effective means of reducing cognitive load because they help to externalise and capture transient information and subsequently free up space in working memory.

What are the main types of word diagrams?

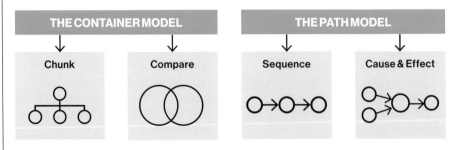

Read More: *Organise Ideas* by Oliver Caviglioli and David Goodwin

How do I implement them?

Develop advanced organisers:
Advanced organisers are tools that prepare students for new learning. The container model aids in visualising relevant information in order to tap into students' existing knowledge. For example, before teaching *Of Mice and Men*, an English teacher might show the organiser opposite to help students understand the notion of 'loneliness' before they start the novel. This paired with a verbal explanation makes this pre-information more tangible and creates a bridge between existing knowledge and the new material.

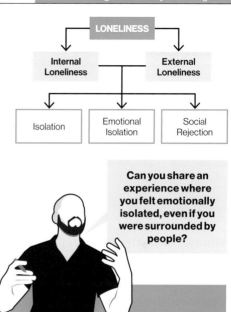

Can you share an experience where you felt emotionally isolated, even if you were surrounded by people?

Live model the process: Following the explanation of a concept, use a visualiser to live model and create a word diagram to represent the new information. Externalise your thinking and ask questions throughout: 'What sections do I need?', 'What order should this be in?', 'What comes first?'. The aim is for students learn how to connect new information to existing knowledge and organise these ideas in a hierarchy or sequence.

Utilise word diagrams to scaffold writing: Developed by Dr. Fred Jones, Visual Instruction Plans (VIPs) are path model word diagrams that help to scaffold a step-by-step process. For example, a flow-spray diagram can be used to deconstruct a writing task into a clear sequence. Providing supporting sentence starters, key vocabulary and instructions build confidence and fluency.

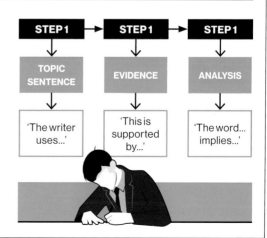

Building Knowledge

Self-Explanation

Repeat, connect and actively integrate knowledge

What is it and why is it effective?

Self-explanation is a process where students explain to themselves verbally or in written form (without notes). It is an effective learning strategy because students not only repeat new information but connect it to what they already understand. In other words, it enables students to actively integrate new information into existing cognitive schemas to create webs of connected knowledge. Self-explaining also leverages the power of retrieval practice. As students explain the concept, they are retrieving the information from long-term memory which strengthens memories, making them more accessible later. Setting short self-explanation tasks encourages meaningful processing and allows teachers to formatively assess students' understanding. Additionally, this strategy fosters metacognitive awareness because children actively synthesis information.

JOHN DUNLOSKY

Self-explanation improves memory, comprehension and problem solving.
(et al 2015)

How do I implement it?

Scaffold and structure: To develop students' ability to implement self-explanation effectively, provide a set of sentence starters or questions. The human brain is naturally wired to remember stories (Willingham 2010) as they provide a framework that aids memory retention. When students rehearse by self-explaining, provide a loose narrative framework, with a clear beginning, middle and end for them to follow.

What is the main concept?

How are these ideas connected?

Read More: *Understanding How We Learn: A Visual Guide* by Yana Weinstein and Megan Sumeracki

The Feynman technique: Named after Nobel Prize-winning physicist Richard Feyman, this technique engages students in an iterative process of self and peer explanation. By engaging them in active recall and teaching, it helps to deepen their understanding, reinforce memory and uncover areas needing further study. Here is how to use the technique with students:

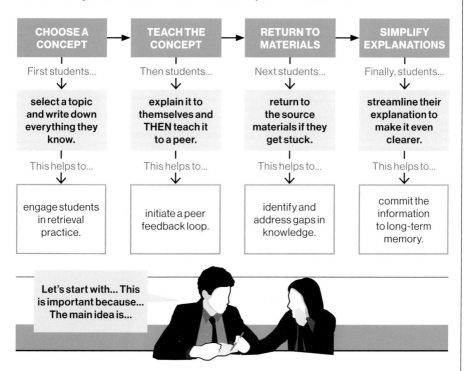

CHOOSE A CONCEPT	TEACH THE CONCEPT	RETURN TO MATERIALS	SIMPLIFY EXPLANATIONS
First students...	Then students...	Next students...	Finally, students...
select a topic and write down everything they know.	explain it to themselves and THEN teach it to a peer.	return to the source materials if they get stuck.	streamline their explanation to make it even clearer.
This helps to...	This helps to...	This helps to...	This helps to...
engage students in retrieval practice.	initiate a peer feedback loop.	identify and address gaps in knowledge.	commit the information to long-term memory.

Let's start with... This is important because... The main idea is...

Get students to teach peers:
Teaching others is a form of peer explanation that helps students to reinforce their learning. Studies show that when students prepare to teach, they recall more information, use better learning strategies, and demonstrate increased effort and motivation (Chase et al 2009). Teachers must be mindful to circulate the classroom during these tasks as there is scope for students to unintentionally spread and embed misconceptions.

Harness technology:
By recording short tutorial videos, students capture their explanations of a topic and support it with simple graphics. Sharing this digitally with others enables them to receive constructive feedback to help them improve. Moreover, students can use Artificial Intelligence (AI) as their audience and prompt it to explain a topic. Subsequently, students identify and explain to the AI what it got wrong or missed (InnerDrive, nd,a).

| Secure Attention | Working Memory | Building Knowledge | **Cognitive Engagement** | Generative Processes |

Cognitive Engagement

Drive thinking in all students and assess knowledge retention in long-term memory

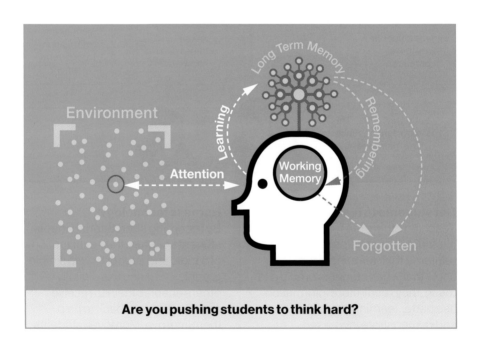

Are you pushing students to think hard?

As mentioned earlier, for new knowledge to be encoded in long-term memory, we must drive *thinking* and ensure that students are cognitively engaged throughout the lesson. On top of this, it is our job to find out what students know. If we don't do this, we can easily fall into the trap of judging students' competence and understanding on a handful of individuals (we all know them), which then develops chasms of unhelpful knowledge gaps. Questioning strategies and formative assessment techniques are sure-fire methods in eliciting evidence of progress that shape our decision making. Furthermore, feedback also plays a critical role supporting students with evaluating knowledge because it helps to ensure that the information being stored in long-term memory is accurate. The following one-pagers involve:

- **Accountability and participation strategies to promote thinking.**
- **Eliciting evidence of student learning.**
- **Formative assessment strategies to move learners forward.**

Cognitive engagement overlaps

The one-pagers in this section overlap with others and can arguably be applied to other aspects of Willingham's Simple Model of the Mind.

	Securing Attention	Working Memory	Building Knowledge	Generative Processes
Formative Assessment		✓	✓	
Checking for Understanding	✓		✓	
Cold Calling	✓		✓	
Think, Pair, Share	✓		✓	✓
Mini-Whiteboards	✓	✓		✓
Hinge Questions		✓		✓
Whole Class Feedback		✓	✓	✓
Peer Critique			✓	✓
Exit Tickets	✓	✓	✓	
Digital Technology		✓	✓	✓

Cognitive Engagement

Formative Assessment

Five responsive strategies to move learners forward

What is it and why is it important?

Formative assessment is central to effective and responsive teaching. It involves the use of strategies aimed at gathering information about students' progress so that teachers can adapt their teaching accordingly and guide students with clear steps for improvement. In *Embedding Formative Assessment* (2015), Wiliam and Leahy outline five key strategies that underpin the effective implementation of formative assessment. They offer a variety of practical tips and adaptations for each strategy, assisting teachers in making informed instructional choices on a daily and moment-to-moment basis. The following table outlines the roles teachers, peers and learners play in the formative assessment process as described by Wiliam and Leahy.

	Where the learner is going	Where the learner is now	How the learner will get there
Teacher	1. Clarifying, sharing and understanding learning intentions and success criteria	2. Engineering effective discussions, tasks and activities that elicit evidence of learning	3. Providing feedback that moves learners forward
Peer		4. Activating students as learning resources for one another	
Learner		5. Activating students as owners of their own learning	

Read More: *Wiliam & Leahy's Five Formative Assessment Strategies in Action* by Kate Jones

How do I implement it?

1 **Clarify success criteria:** Plan and script learning intentions to describe students' learning goals. Learning intentions should be supported by descriptive success criteria so that teachers and students can evaluate performance. Link learning intentions with anonymous samples of student work to help them see what high-quality looks like.

2 **Eliciting evidence:** Eliciting evidence of what students can do is valuable for informed decision-making in the teaching process. Planning quality questions with colleagues enhances the design of effective questions and tasks to promote thinking. Implement no-hands-up approaches to get whole class responses. For example, encourage active participation with cold calling.

3 **Feedback to improve the learner:** Wiliam and Leahy (2015) stress that 'feedback should be more work for the recipient than the donor'. This implies that feedback should be clear, helpful and actionable with the intention of improving the learner. Provide comment only feedback on key pieces of work and dedicate subsequent class time for students to respond.

4 **Activating students as learning resources:** Offer opportunities for students to support each other through the learning process. Scaffolded peer feedback can be highly effective – for example, employing 'two stars and a wish' criteria. Ensure individual accountability in group tasks by carefully assigning specific roles within the group.

DYLAN WILIAM

Dialogue with the teacher provides the opportunity for the teacher to respond to and reorient a pupil's thinking. (et al 1998)

5 **Activating students as owners of their own learning:** Our ultimate objective is to nurture confident lifelong learners who can flourish beyond the confines of the classroom. Equip students with a repertoire of metacognitive strategies to enable them to plan, monitor and evaluate their own learning.

Cognitive Engagement

Checking for Understanding

Assess students' understanding in real-time

What is it and why is it important?

Checking for Understanding (CFU) is a crucial component of effective teaching. It involves teachers regularly assessing what students know about the material being taught. Checking for understanding acts as a tool for teachers to adjust their teaching methods and improve learning by assessing student understanding in real time, allowing them to make necessary instructional decisions such as whether re-teaching during the lesson. Coupled with this, CFU enables a more responsive classroom, fostering a culture of continuous feedback and improvement.

BARAK ROSENSHINE

Checking for student understanding at each point can help students learn the material with fewer errors. (2012)

What does Rosenshine say about CFU?

Barak Rosenshine (2012) asserts that effective teaching involves asking questions and checking students' responses to help them practice new information and connect it with their prior knowledge. Rosenshine's research suggests that teachers should ask questions during instruction to facilitate the practice of new material. The most effective teachers engage all students by having them share answers with peers, summarise points, write responses, or express agreement with others. CFU is key to ensure that the knowledge being transferred to long-term memory is correct.

Read More: 'Five Ways to: Check for Understanding' blog by Tom Sherrington

How do I implement it?

Use a range of questioning: A straightforward and effective method for assessing student knowledge is through questioning. Teachers can employ various questioning strategies to check understanding. These include cold calling students and asking follow up questions to probe their knowledge: 'Why do you think that is?'. Elaborative interrogation questions such as 'Why is this true?' are also powerful to check the depth of students' understanding and help them connect their knowledge to existing schema.

Provide choice statements: Present students with a few choice statements or questions and ask them select a response. For example, 'true or false', 'agree or disagree' and share it via a mini-whiteboard, or hand signal (thumbs up or down). This technique is especially useful in gauging students' prior knowledge or potential misconceptions before beginning new instruction. It also encourages learners to elaborate on the material and make connections to other learning in their long-term memory.

Correcting exercises: A highly efficient and effective method for checking students' understanding is through identifying and rectifying errors and misconceptions. Present an incorrect example and ask students to correct it individually or in pairs. Circulate the room and check for understanding.

Do you agree or disagree with...

What is wrong with this sentence...? Why?

Create visual representations: Graphic organisers and concept maps can be useful for checking the depth of students' understanding. Encourage students to create a visual or symbolic representation (for example a graphic organiser, simple table, or concept map) of information and abstract concepts,

and then have them prepare to discuss their graphics with a partner. Picturing techniques are useful to see if students understand how various concepts or elements of a process are related. It is important to model and rehearse this process so that students know how to create effective visual maps independently.

Cognitive Engagement

Cold Calling

Actively engage all students in the thinking process

DOUG LEMOV

A cold call is an invitation to a student to join a conversation. We want students to be constantly thinking and feel accountable. If we socialise them to think, they'll be more likely to learn. (2010)

What is it and why is it effective?

Cold calling (a strategy developed by Doug Lemov in *Teach Like a Champion*) is used to engage students and encourage active participation from everyone in the class. It involves the teacher strategically selecting students to answer questions or provide responses, rather than relying on volunteers or students who raise their hands. The teacher 'calls' on students without advance notice, which creates a more inclusive and participatory learning environment. Cold calling ensures that all students are actively involved in retrieval practice and that they are held accountable for their understanding and participation. It can be a valuable tool for promoting thinking, preparing all students to contribute, and preventing a small group of students from dominating classroom interactions.

How do I introduce cold calling?

1 Explain the rationale for cold calling to the class before implementing it and rehearse the process so that students become familiar with it.

2 Lemov explains cold calling is not about catching students out. It is about encouraging participation from all students and should be friendly, warm and inviting.

3 Plan and script key questions to make them desirably difficult. Decide the modes of participation (think, pair, share/show-me boards) you will use in advance.

Read More: *Teach Like a Champion 3.0* by Doug Lemov

How do I implement it?

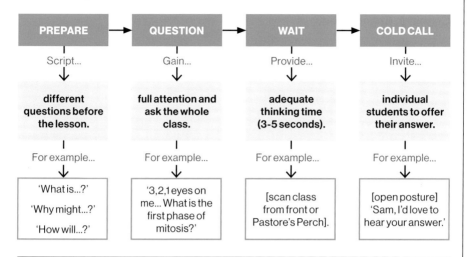

PREPARE	QUESTION	WAIT	COLD CALL
Script...	Gain...	Provide...	Invite...
different questions before the lesson.	full attention and ask the whole class.	adequate thinking time (3-5 seconds).	individual students to offer their answer.
For example...	For example...	For example...	For example...
'What is...?' 'Why might...?' 'How will...?'	'3,2,1 eyes on me... What is the first phase of mitosis?'	[scan class from front or Pastore's Perch].	[open posture] 'Sam, I'd love to hear your answer.'

How do I make sure everyone is thinking? (Tayler 2021)

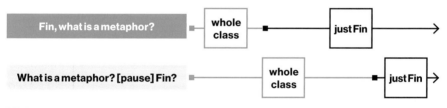

Fin, what is a metaphor? — whole class — just Fin →

What is a metaphor? [pause] Fin? — whole class — just Fin →

What are some effective adaptations?

Written Responses: To reduce anxiety of being called upon, encourage students to jot down their answers to the question in their books or on mini-whiteboards before sharing with the class.

Tip-Off: Before asking a question, tip off which student (or group of students) you'd like to answer. For instance, 'John and Amir, and Emily and Kiara; I'm going to ask both pairs about the faces on 3D shapes. Watch this example...'

Think, Pair, Share: Create a safe, low-stakes space for students to make mistakes before you cold call. TPS allows students to rehearse an idea before sharing and reduces students' anxiety.

TOM SHERRINGTON

If students don't think, they can't learn. Cold calling as a routine is the most effective way to maximise thinking. (2021a)

Cognitive Engagement

Think, Pair, Share

Drive thinking with structured paired discussion

What is it and why is it effective?

Think, Pair, Share (TPS) is an effective strategy for fostering communication and deep thinking. TPS is a routine that should be carried out in three stages. During the 'Think' stage, each student thinks about the question individually and is encouraged to take notes in silence. In the 'Pair' stage, students pair up to exchange and discuss their ideas. Finally, in the 'Share' stage, students share their rehearsed ideas with the entire class. TPS not only enhances students' understanding through collaboration but also promotes active listening and respect for diverse peer perspectives.

COLLABORATION	CONFIDENCE	ACCOUNTABILITY
TPS boosts problem solving and reasoning skills as students have to listen to alternate perspectives and ideas.	TPS builds confidence because students feel heard and validated by peers. It also helps increase participation.	TPS makes students accountable so that everyone is engaged in thinking and have rehearsed answers.

How do I implement it?

Establish routines and use scaffolds:
Strong routines are essential for TPS. Acquaint students with the process by introducing scaffolds or sentence stems (like in the example). Additionally, provide time frames and write a clear focus question (or statement) on the board to help students have deeper, longer and more focused discussions.

That's a valid point Sonia, I wonder if we can take it further by thinking more about...

Read More: *Teaching & Learning Illuminated: The Big Ideas* by Bradley Busch et al

Make TPS a responsive and inclusive process:

A teacher's role during the 'Think' and 'Pair' stages is to observe student discussions and check for understanding. During interactions with students, support them by asking guiding questions or probe them to extend their ideas further. For example, 'Can you explain why you think...?'. Inform students that pairs will be randomly chosen to share their points later. Holding students to this level of accountability helps to encourage them to think, engage and prepare well rehearsed responses that are validated by their peers.

BRADLEY BUSCH

TPS helps build on traditional classroom questioning and help facilitate an open and warm environment.
(et al, nd)

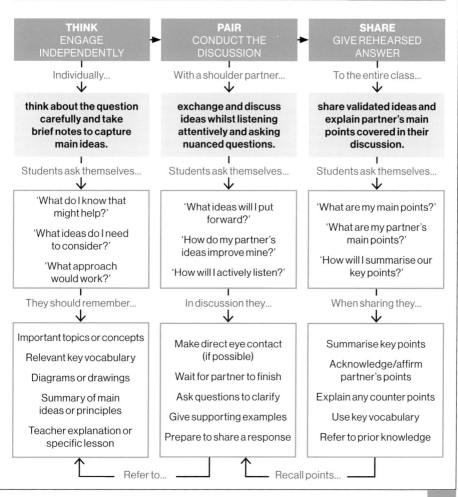

THINK	PAIR	SHARE
ENGAGE INDEPENDENTLY	CONDUCT THE DISCUSSION	GIVE REHEARSED ANSWER
Individually...	With a shoulder partner...	To the entire class...
think about the question carefully and take brief notes to capture main ideas.	**exchange and discuss ideas whilst listening attentively and asking nuanced questions.**	**share validated ideas and explain partner's main points covered in their discussion.**
Students ask themselves...	Students ask themselves...	Students ask themselves...
'What do I know that might help?' 'What ideas do I need to consider?' 'What approach would work?'	'What ideas will I put forward?' 'How do my partner's ideas improve mine?' 'How will I actively listen?'	'What are my main points?' 'What are my partner's main points?' 'How will I summarise our key points?'
They should remember...	In discussion they...	When sharing they...
Important topics or concepts Relevant key vocabulary Diagrams or drawings Summary of main ideas or principles Teacher explanation or specific lesson	Make direct eye contact (if possible) Wait for partner to finish Ask questions to clarify Give supporting examples Prepare to share a response	Summarise key points Acknowledge/affirm partner's points Explain any counter points Use key vocabulary Refer to prior knowledge

Refer to... Recall points...

Cognitive Engagement

Mini-Whiteboards

Drive thinking by getting all students to respond

What are they and why are they effective?

Mini-whiteboards (MWBs) are small, erasable whiteboards used to increase student engagement and participation. They enable teachers to pose questions or problems to the entire class so students can write individual responses. Students then display their answers, allowing teachers to quickly assess understanding and adjust instruction accordingly. MWBs are a low-stakes method of collecting valuable data for an entire class in a short amount of time. As students respond to questions on their whiteboards, teaches can instantly tailor or adjust your questions based on their responses. Due to their transient nature, MWBs give students a safe space to make mistakes and practise new learning.

ADAM BOXER

To make sure your students are ready to practise, use mini whiteboards. (Barton 2022a)

What rules can I use to establish MWB routines?

1 Place the boards on top of your work so you are ready to use them when needed.

2 Keep your answer hidden from others so your teacher knows who needs help.

3 Only start writing when your teacher says the command word (*3, 2, 1, show me!*).

4 Write in large, clear writing so your teacher can see your answers from the front.

5 Write your answer then put down your pen. Place MWB face down on the desk.

6 Your teacher will signal to let you all know when to hold up your response.

How do I implement them?

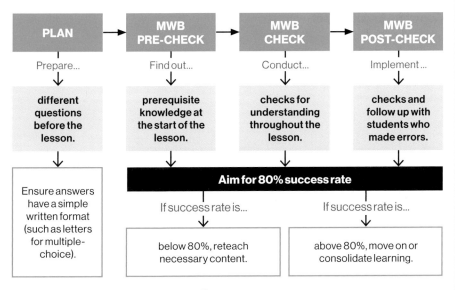

PLAN	MWB PRE-CHECK	MWB CHECK	MWB POST-CHECK
Prepare...	Find out...	Conduct...	Implement...
different questions before the lesson.	**prerequisite knowledge at the start of the lesson.**	**checks for understanding throughout the lesson.**	**checks and follow up with students who made errors.**

Ensure answers have a simple written format (such as letters for multiple-choice).

Aim for 80% success rate

If success rate is...

below 80%, reteach necessary content.

If success rate is...

above 80%, move on or consolidate learning.

Stagger and scan: Strategically stagger student responses to scan and check as many MWBs as possible. If the class is seated in rows, check answers row by row starting from back to front to minimise the chance of copying, opting-out or answer changing.

Capture precise data: Carefully plan and rehearse questions before the lesson. Questions requiring short answers are most effective as they can be observed easily from the front. Aim for questions with brief 1–5 word responses targeting common misconceptions. Mix up the format of your questions. For example, MCQs, yes or no, fill the blank, draw a diagram.

Give live feedback during the MWB process: Giving feedback after retrieval practice has shown to improve learning. During the checking process, give short, sharp feedback to each student prompting them to perform an instant action. For example, 'Jack, check your use of decimal places. Go to your notes to help you make the necessary adjustment'.

Cognitive Engagement

Hinge Questions

Identify and respond to common misconceptions

What are they and why are they effective?

A hinge question is a pivotal diagnostic tool in a learning sequence, used to evaluate students' grasp of the content being taught. It should be carefully planned and crafted to assesses students' understanding of the lesson's objectives and enable the teacher to make informed decisions about their next steps, whether to move forward, revisit, or adjust their teaching. Designed to be presented in a multiple-choice format, hinge questions often include plausible distractors to identify and address common misconceptions and collate immediate feedback from the entire class.

DYLAN WILIAM

The important point is that you do not know what to do until the evidence of students' achievement is elicited... the lesson hinges on this point. (Wiliam and Leahy, 2015)

How do I implement them?

Plan and develop quality questions: In any given unit of work, anticipate and identify the most common misconceptions students might have. Use this information to shape your hinge questions. As Dylan Wiliam (2015) notes, 'Good questions are never finalised. They are always a work in progress.' This suggests that hinge questions should be continually revisited and revised to ensure students are providing the correct response for the right reasons. It is good practice to check students' answers by asking them to explain their choices after each hinge question.

Read More: *Responsive Teaching* by Harry Fletcher-Wood

Design each answer to reflect one misconception: To precisely identify what students are thinking, each incorrect answer (distractor) should be plausible, make sense and reflect a misconception that is directly related to the key learning goal of the lesson. Each distractor in the question opposite is plausible because it reflects common misunderstandings about atmospheric science and the role of different gases in the atmosphere.

What is the primary role of the greenhouse gases in Earth's atmosphere?

↓

A	To provide oxygen for breathing.
B	To protect Earth from harmful solar radiation.
C	To trap heat and keep Earth's surface warm. ✓

Utilise the four part process: Assessing using hinge questions encompasses preparation, execution, analysis and follow-up actions:

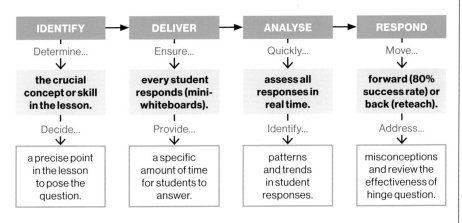

IDENTIFY	DELIVER	ANALYSE	RESPOND
Determine...	Ensure...	Quickly...	Move...
↓	↓	↓	↓
the crucial concept or skill in the lesson.	every student responds (mini-whiteboards).	assess all responses in real time.	forward (80% success rate) or back (reteach).
Decide...	Provide...	Identify...	Address...
↓	↓	↓	↓
a precise point in the lesson to pose the question.	a specific amount of time for students to answer.	patterns and trends in student responses.	misconceptions and review the effectiveness of hinge question.

Lead discussion: Students think hardest when they are uncertain of the correct answer. After the hinge question, refrain from giving the answer straight away. Research (D'Mello et al 2014) suggests that an element of confusion helps students remember the correct answer. Leading the discussion and listening to interpretations from the class before revealing the right response can unearth unexpected misconceptions. To do this, ask students to compare the similarities and differences between answers and discuss with a peer using the 'Think, Pair, Share' or 'Turn and Talk' routine.

HARRY FLETCHER-WOOD

Hinge questions are a fantastic way to understand student understanding.
(2013)

Cognitive Engagement

Whole Class Feedback

Offer actionable feedback and reduce workload

DAISY CHRISTODOULOU

Feedback should... improve pupils' thinking. For whole class feedback to be more effective, it has to move from a statement to a specific action. (2019)

What is it and why is it effective?

Whole class feedback (WCF) involves providing formative feedback to an entire class or group of students on their overall performance, rather than giving individual feedback to each student. This type of feedback is typically delivered through a structured template and can help to create a shared understanding of learning outcomes. WCF is particularly useful for teachers because it helps to reduce workload, save time and inform planning. Conducted in class, WCF is more likely to generate important discussions where teachers can unpick common misconceptions. As with all feedback, it's essential to provide students with concrete steps for action, critical in advancing their learning.

What do I include in my WCF?

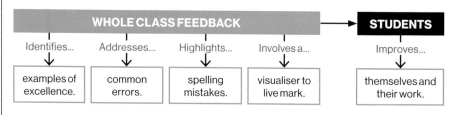

WHOLE CLASS FEEDBACK				STUDENTS
Identifies...	Addresses...	Highlights...	Involves a...	Improves...
examples of excellence.	common errors.	spelling mistakes.	visualiser to live mark.	themselves and their work.

Read More: '6 Steps to Effective Whole-Class Feedback' blog by Andrew Atherton

How do I implement them?

Use the 'Defining Excellence' approach: English teacher, Andrew Atherton's approach to WCF involves identifying examples of excellence in students' work and modelling what it looks like. Andy's seven steps to WCF are:

ANDREW ATHERTON

Andrew's 'Defining Excellence' (2021) method involves deconstructing common misconceptions under a visualiser and culminates in a 'Together Task' addressing the different strands of the feedback. A key focus is getting students to replicate and develop excellence in their own work.

1	Highlight examples of what you liked.
2	Find the common misconceptions.
3	Pinpoint examples of excellence.
4	Create and share a template.
5	Get students to look at your highlighting.
6	Live model the examples of excellence.
7	Do a 'Together Task' based on WCF.

Discuss feedback with class: After reviewing students' work, make your whole class feedback method visible. Use a simple template to record students' main successes and areas for improvement. This might mean using bullet points to summarise minor errors or examples from students' work to illustrate what excellence looks like. Present your feedback to the class using a visualiser or on a PowerPoint slide.

Make feedback actionable: Dylan Wiliam (2000) emphasises that for feedback to be effective, it must provide 'a recipe for future action'. This means feedback written as vague descriptive statements are meaningless and do not prompt cognitive work or specifically address misconceptions. For example, an English teacher might write: 'Develop your use of figurative language.' Instead, they could write: 'Find where you have used a similes instead of metaphors and turn them into metaphors about the scene.'

Cognitive Engagement

Peer Critique

Structure 'kind', 'specific' and 'helpful' peer feedback

What is it and why is it effective?

Peer-to-peer critique can help students appreciate that their learning and understanding is not fixed, it develops. Ron Berger's powerful approach to peer critique helps students to process success criteria, consider models and give 'kind', 'specific' and 'helpful' feedback to their peers. When students help each other improve their work, they are able to give and receive feedback and in the process internalise success criteria to make subsequent improvements. This process helps students to secure their learning in long-term memory so that it can be retrieved easier later.

DYLAN WILIAM

Engaging students in assessing the work of their peers... can substantially increase student achievement. (2015)

Activate students as learning resources for each other: Dylan Wiliam explains that teachers should provide students with opportunities to support each other through the learning process. Peer feedback is particularly powerful when scaffolded effectively – for example, using a resource to scaffold supportive language or using 'two stars and a wish' criteria. In group tasks, ensure individual accountability by giving specific group roles to each student. For example, do not assign a student as a 'reporter' until the end of the work. Implementing structured Think, Pair, Share routines or peer-to-peer quizzing can offer valuable chances for student dialogue and collaborative challenge.

Read More: *Berger's An Ethic of Excellence in Action* by Sonia Thompson

How do I implement it?

 K **Students must be kind:** Encourage students to offer kind feedback to each other. Use scaffolds to train students how to give, receive and process constructive criticism.

S **Students must be specific:** Using success criteria, students must be able to pinpoint specific successes in their partner's work and identify potential improvements.

H **Students must be helpful:** Students should be able to give helpful and actionable feedback. Model how to give feedback and suggest ways it can actionable.

RON BERGER

Build a place where critique is welcome.... Eventually the culture of critique permeates the classroom and informal critique starts taking place all the time. (2003)

How can I scaffold peer critique with students?

BE KIND GIVE THOUGHTFUL PRAISE	BE SPECIFIC GIVE PRECISE FEEDBACK	BE HELPFUL GIVE ACTIONABLE GUIDANCE
Students ask 'what..?' ↓	Students ask 'what..?' ↓	Students ask 'how..?' ↓
'What did they do particularly well?' **'What success criteria was achieved?'**	**'What part needs improvement?'** **'What is their work missing?'**	**'How would I improve the work?'** **'What steps can I suggest?'**
Students use praise... ↓	Students focus on... ↓	Students refer to... ↓
'You effectively showed...' 'You beautifully demonstrated...'	Vocabulary Use of techniques Analysis of evidence	Model answers Success criteria Teacher examples
Be positive & encouraging... ↓	Be honest & precise... ↓	Be clear & constructive... ↓
'I really liked the way you used... to...' 'The most successful part is... because...'	'In the first/second/third paragraph...' 'An idea that needs developing is...'	'To improve, add/rewrite... so that...' 'Try changing... so that...'

Exit Tickets

Assess learning and collect formative data

DOUG LEMOV

You'll know how effective your lesson was, as measured by how well they learned it, not how well you thought you taught it. (2010)

What are they and why are they effective?

Exit tickets are an effective method for assessing understanding at the end of a lesson. The idea is that they provide a low-stakes opportunity to test students on new knowledge aligning with the main learning objectives. Exit tickets can be used daily or weekly, depending on the unit being taught. They buy teachers the time to gain valuable insights into where students are at and if they have a grasp of the material taught. Collecting data on prevalent misconceptions and errors is invaluable to inform planning and influence the direction of teaching.

How do I implement them?

Write simple multiple-choice questions:
Before students leave the lesson, pose a question focused on the learning intention. Simple multiple-choice questions work effectively. For example, after teaching a lesson on the causes of WWI, a question could be:

Which event marked the start of World War I?

A) The assassination of Franz Ferdinand

B) The signing of the Treaty of Versailles

C) The Battle of Stalingrad

Respond to exit ticket data: As educator and author, Harry Fletcher-Wood (2019) explains, 'Exit tickets allow responsive teaching'. Collecting and analysing the data of exit tickets empowers teachers to respond to gaps in students' knowledge and address this in subsequent lessons. If questions are focused on learning objectives, the exit ticket should link to the fundamental knowledge that encapsulates the purpose of the lesson. Fletcher-Wood's 'Divide', 'Dig' and 'Decide' acronym is useful to remember when organising and responding to exit ticket data.

HARRY FLETCHER-WOOD

Exit tickets are simple but powerful: designing and using them can help us refine our planning, find out what students have understood and teach more responsively. (2019)

1   **Divide** by splitting exit tickets into three piles: 'Yes', 'No' and 'Maybe'.

2   **Dig** by examining the 'No' and 'Maybe' pile for patterns of errors or misconceptions.

3   **Decide** on the next steps and target misconceptions, or offer more practice.

Exit tickets promote retrieval practice: When students recall what they have learned without textbooks or notes, it produces great long-term memory effects.

Address the data in the next lesson: If exit tickets are designed effectively, it is likely there will be a mix of correct and incorrect responses. Feedback is key to moving learners forward. With this in mind, address the incorrect answers by reteaching material in the starter of the next lesson or sit down with individuals who struggled at an appropriate time.

Collect and manage data efficiently with digital tools: Depending on availability of tech, digital exit tickets can be a useful way of sorting and analysing formative data. Tools such as Poll Everywhere, Microsoft Forms or Google Forms are effective ways to gather information and to provide a visual overview of students' understanding.

Cognitive Engagement

Digital Technology

Embed digital tools to support teaching and learning

What is it and why is it effective?

Introducing technology into the classroom can be exciting. However, it is important that it is used meaningfully to support or enhance teaching and learning. Schools must have a clear vision and plan for the adoption of technology. For example, if feedback is a school focus, tools should be implemented that improve the feedback process – such as speed of delivery (via voice notes or digital annotations). Furthermore, sustainable professional learning helps to ensure the integration of technology has lasting impact.

Video Explanation

Audio Feedback

Interactive Quizzes

AI Tools

What does research from the EEF say? (2021a)

PEDAGOGICAL RATIONALE	QUALITY OF INSTRUCTION	MAXIMISE PRACTICE	ASSESSMENT AND FEEDBACK
Plan and... ↓	Aim to use... ↓	Utilise... ↓	Improve... ↓
consider how technology will improve teaching and learning before introducing it.	technology to improve the quality of instruction, such as explanations and modelling.	digital tools that offers ways to improve the impact of student practice.	and streamline the delivery of assessment and feedback through digital tools.

Read More: *Teachers vs Tech?: The Case for an Ed Tech Revolution* by Daisy Christodoulou

How do I implement it?

Streamline feedback with digital tools: Technology can streamline feedback by providing ways for teachers to record voice notes or to still encourage children to write in their books but then scan and upload their work to a platform that allows teachers to easily access all necessary information in one place. Teachers can then annotate and mark digitally (Clark et al 2022). According to the EEF (2021b), studies of verbal feedback show slightly higher impacts than written feedback overall (+7 months). Screen recording is also an effective way of combining written and audio feedback as it replicates the idea of sitting next to the child in the class.

JAMIE CLARK

Technology should support or enhance instruction. When integrating tech, remember pedagogy first, technology second.

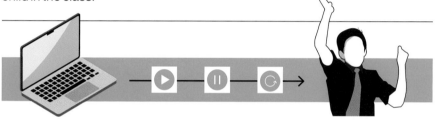

Explain and model with video and visualisers: Utilising video recordings to introduce new content is powerful because it enables students to pause and replay information so they can learn at their own pace. Additionally, video explanations are a cornerstone of 'flipped learning', which is an approach where students are introduced to new material by watching a video prior to the lesson. Perhaps one of the most effective methods of delivering explanations and worked examples in class is using a visualiser to project the teacher's work onto the board live.

Practise with digital quizzes: Interactive quizzing apps and tools (such as Quizizz and Kahoot) are simple ways of quickly and efficiently collecting low-stakes test data on students. Also, Artificial Intelligence (AI) tools like ChatGPT can quickly generate different types of retrieval practice questions.

Work smarter with AI tools: AI can help to provide constructive feedback on students' work. By offering immediate and adaptive responses to projects, assignments and assessments, AI can also analyse individual learning patterns and offer tailored recommendations (Busch et al, nd).

Secure Attention	Working Memory	Building Knowledge	Cognitive Engagement	**Generative Processes**

Generative Processes

Retrieving schema and making lasting connections

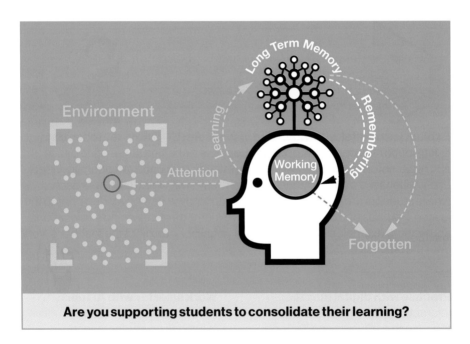

Are you supporting students to consolidate their learning?

When students self-generate knowledge, they actively construct meaningful connections. Neuroscientist Arthur Shimamura (2018) states, 'When we generate information, learned material is reactivated, thus enabling *memory consolidation*.' This notion of consolidation is visualised beautifully by Efrat Furst in her 'Learning a new concept' diagram on the next page. Here, new knowledge (NK) is consolidated into existing knowledge networks (K) through 'active' learning, which occurs when existing connects with new knowledge.

As we have learned so far, effective schema building does not occur in lessons overly focused on activities. Teachers should strive to create opportunities for students to grapple with generative activities and subsequently challenge them to pull information *out* of their heads through spaced retrieval practice activities. The one-pagers in this section focus on:

- **Developing metacognitive and self-regulation strategies.**

- **Strengthening memory with low-stakes retrieval practice tasks.**

Learning a new concept   **K** Knowledge   **NK** New Knowledge

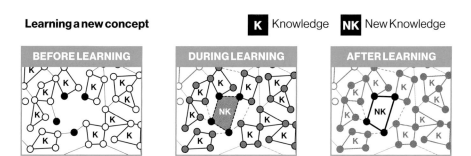

Generative processes overlaps

The one-pagers in this section overlap with others and can arguably be applied to other aspects of Willingham's Simple Model of the Mind.

	Secure Attention	Working Memory	Building Knowledge	Cognitive Engagement
Metacognition				✓
Retrieval Practice			✓	✓
Low-Stakes Recall	✓		✓	✓
Multiple-Choice Questions	✓		✓	✓
Spacing and Interleaving		✓	✓	✓
Review		✓	✓	✓

Generative Processes

Metacognition

Develop students' self-regulation and independence

What is it and why is it important?

A metacognitive learner is one who has awareness of what they are thinking about and has control over their cognitive skills. Teachers can teach practical strategies explicitly to help students self-regulate and choose appropriate pathways when facing different learning challenges. Independent learners have an awareness of generative processes and control their own study strategies to consolidate learning and counter the natural fading of memories. While there is some benefit to introducing students to the general importance of planning, monitoring and evaluating, it's important to note that specific strategies tend to be subject- or task-specific. The Education Endowment Foundation (2021c) highlights that the effectiveness of metacognitive strategies rely on their integration with subject content, suggesting that these strategies are most effectively taught in context with the subject matter. Properly applied, metacognitive strategies the use of metacognitive strategies can be worth the equivalent of an additional +7 months' progress.

How do I implement it?

Ensure it is subject specific: Embed metacognitive instruction within specific subjects to align directly with the tasks at hand. Employing explicit instruction in cognitive and metacognitive strategies can assist students in demystifying and internalising expert thinking (Education Endowment Foundation 2021c). The 7 step method can support with this.

1. Activating prior knowledge
2. Explicit strategy instruction
3. Modelling of learned strategy
4. Memorisation of strategy
5. Guided practice
6. Independent practice
7. Structured reflection

Read More: *The Metacognition Handbook* by Jennifer Webb

Develop metacognitive awareness: Support students to plan, monitor and evaluate their learning by modelling thinking and asking questions.

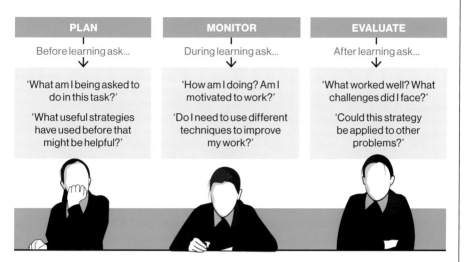

PLAN	MONITOR	EVALUATE
Before learning ask...	During learning ask...	After learning ask...
'What am I being asked to do in this task?'	'How am I doing? Am I motivated to work?'	'What worked well? What challenges did I face?'
'What useful strategies have used before that might be helpful?'	'Do I need to use different techniques to improve my work?'	'Could this strategy be applied to other problems?'

Embed reflection and dialogue: Provide reflection tasks, such as exam wrappers (a post-exam, self-evaluation form), to help students think critically about their learning and how to improve. Moreover, encouraging metacognitive talk in the classroom can assist students in reflecting on their learning. This can be achieved through structured discussions, peer-to-peer teaching, or guided reflection activities, where students analyse the success of their learning approaches. Incorporating activities like think-alouds can further support metacognitive awareness.

ALEX QUIGLEY

We should also train our pupils to better plan, monitor and evaluate their own learning, so that when face situations like sitting down and staring at a blank exam paper, they can apply their learning with success. (2018)

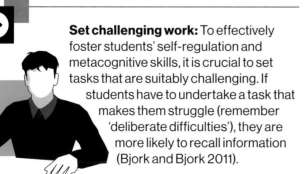

Set challenging work: To effectively foster students' self-regulation and metacognitive skills, it is crucial to set tasks that are suitably challenging. If students have to undertake a task that makes them struggle (remember 'deliberate difficulties'), they are more likely to recall information (Bjork and Bjork 2011).

Generative Processes

Retrieval Practice

Strengthen memory retention and boost learning

What is it and why is it important?

Retrieval practice is a learning strategy whereby learned information is recalled from memory. The act of retrieving information boosts learning as we are challenged to think about what we know. This process not only identifies gaps in knowledge but also strengthens memory over time. Effective low-stakes retrieval practice tasks include flashcards, brain dumps, past papers and self and peer quizzing. Unless we regularly retrieve information from long-term memory, we tend to forget what we have learned. Retrieval practice is important because it enables students to revisit what they have learned, ensuring it is not forgotten and can be used as a foundation for further learning.

ROBERT BJORK

Using your memory, shapes your memory.
(gocognitive 2012)

How do I implement it?

Educator and author Tom Sherrington (2019a) recommends the following principles when applying retrieval practice regularly with students:

- Involve all students in the retrieval process.
- Make checking answers accurate and easy.
- Specify the knowledge and keep it generative.
- Vary the diet and mix up low-stakes strategies.
- Ensure it is time and workload efficient.

Read More: *Powerful Teaching: Unleash the Science of Learning* by Pooja K. Agarwal and Patrice Bain

How does it link to the Simple Model of the Mind?

Willingham's model helps to explain how retrieval supports learning by understanding the interplay between working memory and long-term memory.

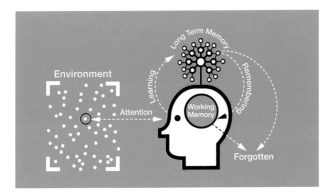

When you practice retrieving information, you are essentially pulling it from long-term memory into working memory. This process strengthens the neural pathways, making the information easier to access the next time you need it. It also helps to identify gaps in your knowledge, which is crucial for effective studying. By repeatedly recalling information, you are reinforcing the memory and helping to move that information from short-term or working memory into long-term memory, a concept known as the 'testing effect' or 'practice testing'.

Distribute practice: Retrieval practice is more effective when conducted in short bursts and spaced over time. Revisiting information after intervals makes retrieval more challenging but leads to higher long-term retention in long-term memory. Spaced practice involves reviewing underlying concepts like vocabulary, formulae or key events.

Interleave topics: Alternate between two or more related concepts or skills instead of focusing entirely on one at a time. When students are exposed to information more frequently, they tend to remember it better. For example, practise Topic A, B and C on alternating days throughout the week.

THE BENEFITS OF RETRIEVAL PRACTICE
(InnerDrive, nd, b)

1. Identifies gaps in knowledge

2. Makes connections

3. Checks for misconceptions

4. Strengthens connections

5. Makes robust connections

6. Makes new learning easier

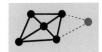

Generative Processes

Low-Stakes Recall

Add variety by hiding the broccoli in the brownies

What is it and why is it important?

Retrieval practice can be quite challenging and feel repetitive if activities are not varied. Cognitive scientist Dr. Megan Sumeracki (2019) coined the catchy phrase 'hiding the broccoli in the brownies', which means it is healthy to mix up low-stakes retrieval practice activities to help keep the recall process fresh. Low-stakes strategies can be not only stand-alone retrieval exercises but also integrated into learning activities. These strategies are effective because they reduce the pressure and anxiety associated with testing, allowing students to focus on the process of retrieval and improvement. When students are not worried about their performance, they are more likely to engage and build confidence.

**MEGAN
SUMERACKI**

It is very possible to hide the broccoli in the brownies by infusing retrieval-based learning into fun activities in the classroom. (2019)

How do I implement it?

Use a variety of low-stakes quizzes: Solely relying on strategies like re-reading or highlighting text can lead to an inaccurate self-assessment of knowledge. Quizzes and practice tests aid students in assessing their grasp of recently learned material, showing strengths and areas for improvement. Administering quizzes immediately after a lesson and revisiting the content throughout the course enhances learning. Try simple paper quizzes or whole class 'show me' quizzes (using mini-whiteboards). Tech tools (such as Quizizz) can be effective in capturing more nuanced data on all students. This information can be used to inform the direction of your teaching.

Read More: *Retrieval Practice: Resources and Research for Every Classroom* by Kate Jones

How does...?

Why might...?

How can...?

Why is...?

Ask 'how' and 'why' questions: Elaborative interrogation focuses on enhancing memory retention by prompting students to generate 'how' and 'why' questions after learning. Once these questions are formulated, students should explore potential answers that elucidate cause-and-effect relationships. When studying photosynthesis, students might ask questions like, 'Why is chlorophyll green?', 'Why is its colour important?' and 'How do plants capture sunlight?'.

KATE JONES

Retrieval practice, like exercise, must be consistent, regular and the level of challenge should be appropriate with desirable difficulties. (2019)

Use free recall and self-explaining: Free recall, also known as brain dump, involves asking students to write down everything they remember relevant to the question (or the topic). Subsequently, you can ask students to compare their work to find gaps, similarities and differences in their understanding. Similarly, self-explaining involves students pulling out information from memory and putting into words or a simple narrative. During this process, students generate their own interpretation of the material and make natural connections between ideas.

Incorrect: move card to previous box

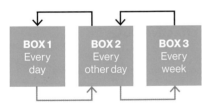

Correct: move card to the next box

Implement flashcards: Flashcards offer a structured, repetitive format that allows students to actively recall information from memory. Mixing up different types of flashcards with multiple-choice or open-ended questions allows students to retrieve information in different contexts. Instruct students how to use the cards properly (by not cheating and looking at the answers) and how to space their practice (every day, every other day or week) using the Leitner System to ensure a systematic approach to learning that builds on the principle of spaced repetition.

Generative Processes

Multiple-Choice Questions

Write questions to assess students with efficiency

What are they and why are they effective?

Multiple-choice questions (MCQs) are an efficient method of assessment as they are simple to deliver and score. They can be used for summative assessment purposes or for low-stakes retrieval activities to formatively assess learning and check for understanding. Multiple-choice questions are concise and can be assessed objectively, minimising bias. Moreover, they offer a versatile format that can be deployed easily within a lesson. When written well, MCQs provide effective retrieval support and can make teaching more responsive to the needs of individual learners.

PATTI SHANK

Multiple-choice questions allow us to efficiently measure a wide range of knowledge and skills and easily and objectively score assessments.

How do I implement effective MCQs?

1	**Avoid using the phrase, 'none of the above'.**
2	**Give three possible answers to MCQs.**
3	**Give helpful formative feedback afterwards.**
4	**Use plausible distractors to promote thinking.**
5	**Support MCQs with clear learning objectives.**
6	**Use simple and concise language.**

Read More: *Write Better Multiple-Choice Questions to Assess Learning* by Patti Shank

How do I implement them?

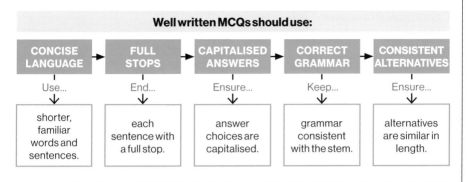

Well written MCQs should use:

CONCISE LANGUAGE	FULL STOPS	CAPITALISED ANSWERS	CORRECT GRAMMAR	CONSISTENT ALTERNATIVES
Use...	End...	Ensure...	Keep...	Ensure...
shorter, familiar words and sentences.	each sentence with a full stop.	answer choices are capitalised.	grammar consistent with the stem.	alternatives are similar in length.

Write clear and focused sentence stems: Effective stems ask about relevant and important knowledge or skills related to the learning objective. They are concise, positively stated and include only relevant details. Furthermore, effective stems must not give away any clues to the correct answer. Evidence shows that the two best formats for stems are a simple question or an incomplete sentence that students need to complete.

Design effective answer choices with plausible distractors: Answer choices for MCQs should be clear, concise and consistent in length and detail. It is important to present answer choices so they appear in logical order. For example, a chronological list of dates or quantities. Furthermore, effective MCQs should include plausible distractors (incorrect answer choices). Good distractors should stem from common errors or misconceptions. Make sure each answer choice is roughly the same length and level of detail because students who are familiar with MCQs use answer length as a hint to the correct answer.

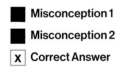

■ Misconception 1

■ Misconception 2

X Correct Answer

Use MCQs as hinge questions: A hinge question serves as a diagnostic tool, strategically placed at crucial junctures in the lesson. Its primary role is to assess student comprehension, enabling you to determine the next steps in instruction. These questions are particularly adept at identifying prevalent misunderstandings and collecting data on student knowledge. Hinge questions should be paired with methods like mini-whiteboards or digital tools, which help to collect whole class responses.

Generative Processes

Spacing and Interleaving

Create conditions that optimise long-term retention

What is it and why is it important?

Spaced practice and interleaving are two learning strategies that enhance memory retention and strengthen learning. Spaced practice involves spreading out study sessions over time, rather than cramming information. On the other hand, interleaving involves mixing up different types of learning (switching different subjects problem types). Spaced practice increases effort to retrieve the information, which improves the durability of learning (Carpenter and Agarwal 2020). Interleaving problems helps students to work out and select and apply correct strategies, helping them improve the brain's ability to discriminate between different types of information. Bjork's research on 'desirable difficulties' outlines reasons why these strategies help students learn more in the long-term and not simply perform well in the short-term.

ROBERT BJORK

Conditions that create challenges and slow the rate of apparent learning often optimize long-term retention. (1994)

How is learning different to performance?

Learning is a change in long-term memory. Without that change, it is just performance.

LEARNING	PERFORMANCE
Invisible (thinking hard)	Observable (engagement)
Long-term improvement	Short-term improvement
Stable	Fragile
Misleading (test results can be underwhelming)	Misleading (test results can be seductive)

Read More: 'Strengthening the Student Toolbox' paper by John Dunlosky

How do I implement it?

Spaced practice: Spacing out learning sessions improves retention over time. The natural enemy of spacing is 'cramming', which often feels fluent and provides high student satisfaction because performance is often high. However, research by Bjork and Bjork shows that people can learn while not (yet) demonstrating improved performance and can perform without having learned anything. Importantly, allowing for some forgetting improves storage strength upon retrieval because it makes retrieval harder.

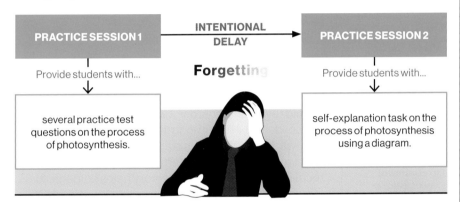

Interleaved practice: Varying different problem types improves retention over time. The natural enemy of interleaving is 'blocking', which gives the learner the illusion of competence that can hurt long-term learning. Mixing up problems means memory is constantly activated and has to 'reload'. This struggle fosters lasting learning. Dunlosky (2013) writes, 'When a new problem is presented, students need to first figure out which kind of problem it is and what steps they need to take to solve it.'

JOHN DUNLOSKY

Distributed practice may take more effort, but it is essential for obtaining knowledge in a manner that will be maintained (or easily relearned) over longer, educationally relevant periods of time. (2013)

Blocking vs Interleaving

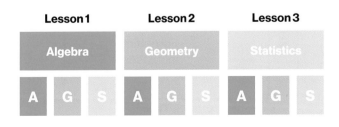

Generative Processes

Review

Reflect on prior learning daily, weekly and monthly

BARAK ROSENSHINE

Begin a lesson with a short review of previous learning: daily review can strengthen previous learning and can lead to fluent recall. (2012)

What is it and why is it important?

Barak Rosenshine (2012) suggests that teachers should review material daily, weekly and monthly to consolidate learning in long-term memory. For daily reviews, he recommends starting a lesson with a short review of previous learning. The process of recalling information from memory helps students to strengthen memory traces, increasing the chance of the information being more accessible later on. With consistent practice, learning becomes automatic thereby freeing up more space in working memory for students to learn new things. Having a variety of retrieval practice activities up your sleeve makes reviewing more engaging and lets students activate prior knowledge in different ways.

Strengthening memories:

Because memories tend to fade over time, use daily, weekly and monthly review to ensure more information is continually refreshed and consolidated in long-term memory (InnerDrive, nd, c).

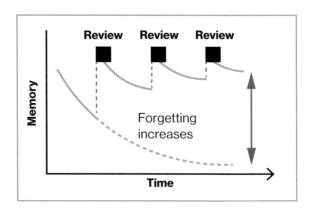

Read More: 'Why Daily, Weekly and Monthly Reviews Matter' blog by InnerDrive

How do I implement it?

Conduct daily reviews: Begin lessons with a five-to eight-minute review of previously covered material. Rosenshine (2012) explains that highly effective teachers reviewed vocabulary, formulae, events, or previously learned concepts. These teachers gave opportunities for additional practice on facts and skills that were needed for recall to become automatic. Retrieval practice activities are also effective for daily review. These include brief multiple-choice quizzes, flashcards and short written paragraphs.

Include misconceptions: Weed out common misconceptions by including them in your review activities. For example, adding misconceptions to quizzes or teacher example paragraphs. As noted by InnerDrive (nd, c), Rosenshine didn't necessarily equate 'review' with 'quizzing'. He also recommended it encompass correcting homework, revisiting concepts and skills that students have applied and identifying areas of difficulty, thereby providing opportunities for support and further practice.

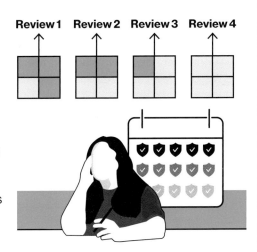

Review 1   Review 2   Review 3   Review 4

Engage students in weekly and monthly reviews: Spacing out learning review activities weekly and monthly helps students to improve retention over time. Weekly reviews provide an opportunity to connect the dots between various topics, identifying overarching themes and addressing recurring misconceptions. Monthly reviews act as a comprehensive overview, allowing students to zoom out and reflect on their learning progress.

Rosenshine recommends to...

1. Review and correct homework.
2. Review skills from homework.
3. Review the common errors.
4. Review the difficult questions.
5. Review what needs practising.

Summary

Perhaps the most important idea Willingham's Simple Model of the Mind teaches us is how educators can best ensure learning happens in their classrooms. By understanding the intricate relationship between working memory and long-term memory, teachers can plan to optimise their instruction and design activities carefully so that learning sticks.

To make it more accessible, I have condensed the main ideas from the Simple Model of the Mind into five straightforward takeaways. These takeaways have underpinned my own planning, teaching and professional development over the past few years, resulting in significant improvements in students' engagement and learning outcomes. Furthermore, the takeaways have made a great poster for my office at school and serve as a constant reminder for teachers in my department.

Takeaway 1: Secure attention

Foster positive attentional habits so that students are listening and cognitively engaged.

Takeaway 2: Working memory

Minimise cognitive load so that students are not overwhelmed by too much information.

Takeaway 3: Building knowledge

Build bodies of knowledge (schema) so that students can make connections to what they already know.

Takeaway 4: Cognitive engagement

Drive thinking from all students so that they process information in working memory ('Memory is the residue of thought').

Takeaway 5: Generative processes

Enhance long-term memory retention so that students can easily draw and build upon existing knowledge.

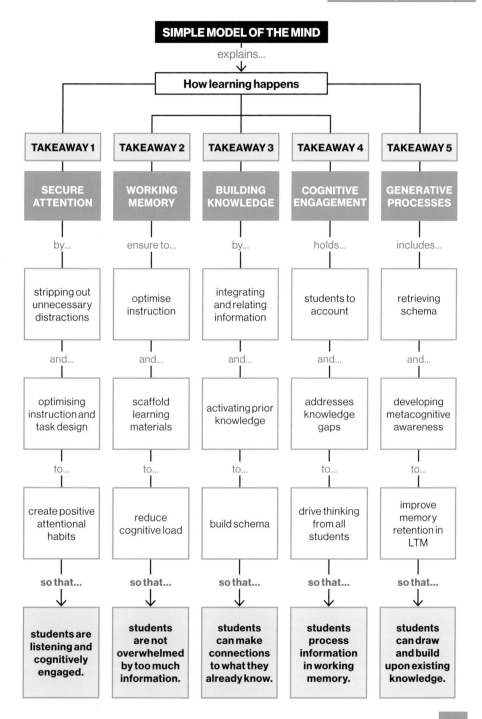

SIMPLE MODEL OF THE MIND

explains...

How learning happens

TAKEAWAY 1	TAKEAWAY 2	TAKEAWAY 3	TAKEAWAY 4	TAKEAWAY 5
SECURE ATTENTION	**WORKING MEMORY**	**BUILDING KNOWLEDGE**	**COGNITIVE ENGAGEMENT**	**GENERATIVE PROCESSES**
by...	ensure to...	by...	holds...	includes...
stripping out unnecessary distractions	optimise instruction	integrating and relating information	students to account	retrieving schema
and...	and...	and...	and...	and...
optimising instruction and task design	scaffold learning materials	activating prior knowledge	addresses knowledge gaps	developing metacognitive awareness
to...	to...	to...	to...	to...
create positive attentional habits	reduce cognitive load	build schema	drive thinking from all students	improve memory retention in LTM
so that...	so that...	so that...	so that...	so that...
students are listening and cognitively engaged.	**students are not overwhelmed by too much information.**	**students can make connections to what they already know.**	**students process information in working memory.**	**students can draw and build upon existing knowledge.**

Expert Teaching Principles:

A collection of one-pagers summarising six expert teaching principles and supporting strategies.

Teaching one Pagers

Expert Teaching Principles

The foundational building blocks of effective teaching

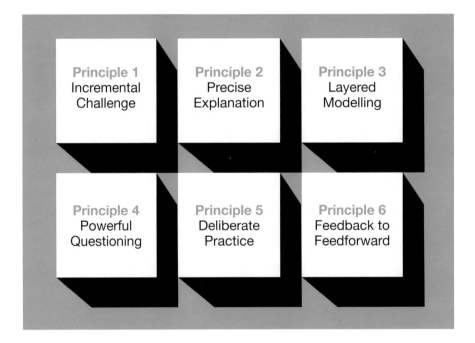

For most teachers, educational literature that demystifies classroom complexities is eagerly welcomed. As with my intention in this book, making pedagogy practical and accessible is a godsend for busy teachers who want to cut out the clutter and focus only on optimising their instruction.

The holy grail for me is the book *Making Every Lesson Count* by Shaun Allison and Andy Tharby (2015). Simply put, it is a gift to the profession because it explains great teaching in its purest form. Much like Sue Hynes (my wise mentor back in 2009), Allison and Tharby speak good old common sense and not only identify six actionable principles for effective teaching and learning (challenge, explanation, modelling, questioning, practice and feedback) but also present a range of concrete strategies to support each principle.

Professor Robert Coe (et al 2014) suggests, 'Great teaching cannot be achieved by following a recipe, but there are some clear pointers in the research to approaches that are most likely to be effective'. *Making Every Lesson Count* is clearly rooted in educational research on effective instruction and takes into account how the mind works, the differences between experts and novices, and cognitive load theory. Looking through this scientific lens, Allison and Tharby's principles are essential building blocks for any school looking to develop a holistic vision for teaching and learning.

In a popular TED Talk, the late Sir Ken Robinson (TED 2007) claims that 'schools kill creativity', arguing that 'we don't grow into creativity, we grow out of it'. Whilst Robinson's ideas are inspiring, I respectfully disagree. From a cognitive science perspective, creativity can be explained as the act of generating new patterns and combinations of *existing* knowledge. According to research, the more knowledge we have, the more new combinations of knowledge we can make. Daniel Willingham (2021) explains that generating new ideas requires divergent thinking; evaluating those ideas for usefulness requires knowledge. So, schools that focus on building knowledge through rich curriculum design and instructional practices are in fact supporting creativity, not killing it.

Managing contemporary evidence-based ideas, curriculum and assessment is a difficult task for any school. *The Learning Rainforest* (2017) by Tom Sherrington wonderfully weaves these ideas together and explores the educational debates about good teaching. In the book, he defines two differing approaches to teaching which he calls 'Mode A and Mode B'. Mode A teaching refers to core instructional

PROFESSOR ROBERT COE

Great teaching cannot be achieved by following a recipe, but there are some clear pointers in the research to approaches that are most likely to be effective. (et al 2014)

PAUL KIRSCHNER

Minimally guided instruction appears to proceed with no reference to the characteristics of working memory... [thus] are highly unlikely to result in effective learning. (et al 2016)

guidance that provides students with a solid foundation of knowledge and skills whilst Mode B teaching relates to off-piste, hands-on activities that 'inspire awe'. These approaches often fall into the binary categories often referred to as 'traditional vs progressive':

'Traditional vs Progressive' Practices (Sherrington 2014)

Traditional

Learning that leans towards an emphasis on content, structures, ordered systems, formal learning and measurable outcomes.

Progressive

Learning that leans towards an emphasis on processes, experiences, discovery, informal learning and intangible outcomes.

**TOM
SHERRINGTON**

Some things only need to be present in very small doses to keep us fit and healthy – but they are still absolutely essential.

Importantly, he argues both Mode A (traditional) and Mode B (progressive) make up the vital ingredients in a student's balanced educational diet. Sherrington writes (2018), 'Some things only need to be present in very small doses to keep us fit and healthy – but they are still absolutely essential.' In other words, whilst Mode B plays an important role in the curriculum, it should not be the bedrock of a school's pedagogical philosophy. This perspective backs up research (Kirschner et al 2006) showing that 'minimally guided instruction (such as discovery, experiential and inquiry-based learning) appears to proceed with no reference to the characteristics of working memory... [thus] are highly unlikely to result in effective learning'. To improve student outcomes, a clear focus must be placed on Mode A instructional methods.

Once schools establish Mode A as the status quo, a little Mode B can be sprinkled throughout the curriculum to take students' knowledge in new and exciting directions. In my own school, we have implemented a dedicated technology course to inspire awe and creativity. It is designed to provide students with the digital skills to apply knowledge by using photography, video, drawing and sound across the curriculum. While this course stands out for its innovation and creative possibilities, its true effectiveness hinges on the robust bedrock of foundational knowledge that students have already acquired.

The good news is that research-based practices have become more common in teaching and learning policies (especially in the UK) in recent years. This can be put down to the influence of cognitive science as well as the rise of movements such as Tom Bennett's ResearchED. A first-class example of this is the Co-op Academy Belle Vue in Manchester in the UK who have developed a collection of guiding principles that form the foundations of quality teaching at their school. Deputy principal Michael Chiles has done a superb job of boiling down the school's pedagogical vision into six teaching principles and their core ingredients. Chiles (2023a) explains that the school works together to 'narrate what each principle looks like in the classroom using our components and active ingredients'. For any school, a collective vision is a North Star for classroom practice and helps teachers to form a shared understanding of what teaching and learning looks like in their classrooms.

The one-pagers in **Collection 2: Expert Teaching Principles** focus on building knowledge and independence through teacher-led instruction and are an amalgamation of Belle Vue's core ingredients and the six teaching and learning principles outlined in *Making Every Lesson Count* (2015). Before you jump into these one-pagers, I recommend that you read the summary of this excellent book on the next page.

Making Every Lesson Count

Six principles to support great teaching and learning

What are Allison and Tharby's six principles of great teaching?

SHAUN ALLISON

Through the application of these six principles, the ultimate goal is to lead students towards independence. (et al 2015)

ANDY THARBY

There are some fundamentals to teaching and learning that we should all be made aware of. (et al 2015)

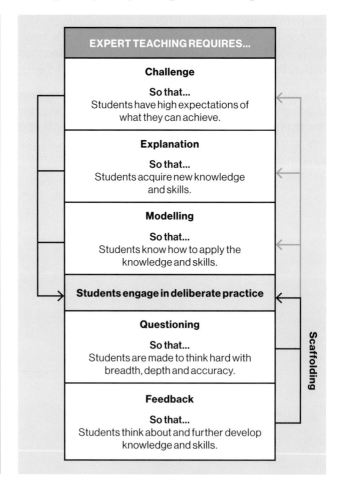

EXPERT TEACHING REQUIRES...

Challenge

So that...
Students have high expectations of what they can achieve.

Explanation

So that...
Students acquire new knowledge and skills.

Modelling

So that...
Students know how to apply the knowledge and skills.

Students engage in deliberate practice

Questioning

So that...
Students are made to think hard with breadth, depth and accuracy.

Feedback

So that...
Students think about and further develop knowledge and skills.

Scaffolding

Challenge: Students should be presented with challenging work to make them think deeply. The skill of an effective teacher is to push all students enough to engage them in 'healthy struggle' and then be responsive to students' needs when necessary.

Explanation: Explanations ought to be linked to something students already know and divided into manageable chunks to avoid overloading working memory. Such explanations help transform abstract ideas into more tangible concepts.

Modelling: To learn how to do something, students need to watch and listen to experts as they guide them through the process. Modelling is the first step on a student's journey towards independence (followed by lots of practice). Research shows that modelling is done best when delivered in small step-by-step blocks using worked examples.

| DEPENDENCE | HEAVY GUIDANCE | LIGHT GUIDANCE | INDEPENDENCE | AUTONOMY |

Practice: Dedicate time for students to practise new material in order to build fluency. This helps to create consolidated knowledge and skills that they can call upon. Students should also engage in deliberate practice, so they are tackling tough material to make them think. Ultimately, without thinking, no learning can occur.

Questioning: Good questions serve to test, deepen and develop one's understanding of a new concept and create a classroom culture of rich discussion. Ensure students engage in cognitive work by using probing questions, involving everyone through cold calling, multiple-choice hinge questions and orchestrating discussion to check for understanding.

Feedback: Teachers should define what students need to aim for, set them off and then keep their learning on track through precise and timely feedback. It is a reciprocal process that aims to close an identified learning gap. Feedback can be verbal, written, given by peers or self-generated. Provide actionable steps and dedicated time for students to edit and improve their work.

| Principle 1 | Principle 2 | Principle 3 | Principle 4 | Principle 5 | Principle 6 |

Incremental Challenge

Expect excellence from all students and make learning desirably difficult so that everyone thinks hard and strives to achieve their best

What is it and why is it important?

Challenge is about having high expectations and engaging all students in difficult problems. Bjork and Bjork's 1994 paper 'Desirable difficulties' focuses on the value of prioritising certain, comparatively difficult learning strategies over others that are more cognitively comfortable. Learning only happens when there is a change in the long-term memory. If we do not get all students to think hard about something, they do not learn it. This means we should plan lessons around what we want students to think about and ensure they are pitched so that they work in the 'struggle zone'. Such learning, though often invisible and long-term, may seem slow and less effective in the short-term. However, this perceived slowness is deceptive; it lays the groundwork for mastery and intellectual resilience.

What are the core ingredients?

EXCELLENT WORK	HEALTHY STRUGGLE	RESPONSIVE
Create a culture of excellence by crafting and drafting work.	Pitch up content so that students are in the zone of healthy struggle.	Provide timely and specific feedback to help students progress.

DESIRABLE DIFFICULTY	HIGH EXPECTATIONS	SELF-REGULATORY
Space and interleave learning to aid long-term memory retention.	Expect excellence from all students to shape productive attitudes.	Use metacognitive strategies to help students self-regulate.

Related Summaries: Retrieval Practice (p.104), Spacing and Interleaving (p.110), Excellent Work (p.146)

How do I implement it?

Effective teachers pitch work perfectly so that it pushes students into the zone of 'healthy struggle' (Alison and Tharby 2015) which makes them think hard.

COMFORT ZONE	STRUGGLE ZONE	PANIC ZONE
↓	↓	↓
Low challenge	High challenge	High challenge
Low stress	Low stress	High stress
Limited thinking	Thinking required	Thinking required
Limited learning	Effective learning	Limited learning

Nurture a culture of excellence: Establish a learning environment where excellence is the norm, adopting attitudes such as, 'only when it's excellent is it complete'. This fosters a mindset where high standards are routinely expected. Motivate students to pursue mastery-oriented goals, where success is measured by their growth and development, rather than just by their grades.

Expect excellence from everyone: Students do not flourish under low expectations. When teachers expect more from their students, they perform better. This self-fulfilling prophecy is known as the Pygmalion Effect (Rosenthal et al 1968). Expecting excellence shapes students' behaviours and attitudes and creates a climate focused on challenge and mastery.

Create 'desirably difficult' learning conditions: Bjork and Bjork's research (1994) suggests that the following strategies help learners to engage in deeper processing, retain information and make connections between concepts:

ROBERT BJORK

In short, try to spend less time on the input side and more time on the output side. (et al 1994)

- Space out your teaching of the same topic over several lessons.

- Interleave (mix up) different topics to help students make connections between them.

- Implement self-testing and retrieval practice activities to strengthen knowledge retention.

| Principle 1 | **Principle 2** | Principle 3 | Principle 4 | Principle 5 | Principle 6 |

Precise Explanation

Artfully weave new information into existing knowledge with clarity and precision so that students can build connected bodies of knowledge

What is it and why is it important?

One of the core elements of a teacher's toolkit is the ability to explain concepts and ideas with clarity and precision. Good teacher talk hinges on having deep subject knowledge and using nuanced language to convey important ideas. Effective teachers not only make explanations engaging but weave in questions to regularly check for understanding. As Daniel Willingham (2010) notes, building background knowledge helps us make sense of new information and link it with what we already know. With this in mind, teacher explanation is a precise and artful way to help students learn underlying factual information, structures and concepts of a particular subject and connect it to prior knowledge and experiences.

What are the core ingredients? (Chiles 2023a)

WEAVE	WORKED EXAMPLES	CREDIBLE
Connect students' new knowledge to their existing knowledge.	Free up working memory by creating step-by-step examples.	Prepare your pitch and deliver the right level of difficulty.

COMBINE	PRECISION	LAYER
Create resources to present information in different ways.	Cut out unnecessary information to minimise distractions.	Gradually fade teacher explanation as students build proficiency.

How do I implement it?

Use concrete examples and non-examples: Illustrate more abstract information with tangible concrete examples. For example, using blocks in a maths lesson. Refer to and deconstruct a series of non-examples to help counter any preexisting misconceptions and errors students may have.

DANIEL WILLINGHAM

The human mind seems exquisitely tuned to understand and remember stories. (2010)

Structure learning like a story: Stories are interesting and have a familiar structure. They contain the 4 Cs (causality, conflict, complications and character) making them more memorable. Design lessons to mimic the narrative flow of a story.

Eye		Camera
Retina	←→	Film
Pupil	←→	Aperture
Lens	←→	Lens
Choroid	←→	Black Paint

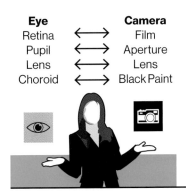

Link ideas using analogies: Here, the 'weave' ingredient comes into play. Analogies act as a bridge, connecting background knowledge with new material to be learned. Start an analogy by reviewing the characteristics of unfamiliar concept with students. Compare the same features in the two concepts and then explain where the analogy breaks down.

The seven steps of preparing for an explanation (Atkins 2023)

1. Set up: Ask yourself key questions about the explanation to clarify the main points you intend to cover.

2. Find the information: Write down all relevant information in one place along with questions students might have.

3. Distill the information: Break information down into small chunks and strip unnecessary information students don't need.

4. Organise the information: Put information into main strands to form a narrative structure.

5. Write the story: Use this structure to formulate a story, applying writing techniques.

6. Tighten: Improve the story by removing potential complications or obstacles to understanding.

7. Delivery: Rehearse the explanation and consider pace, pauses and visual prompts.

Principle 1   Principle 2   **Principle 3**   Principle 4   Principle 5   Principle 6

Layered Modelling

Externalise thinking and show what success looks like in small steps so that students know how to apply new knowledge

What is it and why is it important?

Modelling involves the teacher demonstrating a specific skill, thought, or process for students. The purpose of modelling is to provide a clear and concrete example for students so that they can see what success looks like. Modelling is the first phase of the 'I do, We do, You do' layered process which gradually shifts cognitive work from the teacher to the learner during interactive instruction. As Rosenshine (2012) suggests, the most effective teachers break new information down into small manageable steps and scaffold learning tasks to support novice learners. Modelling centres on providing visual and verbal examples for students to absorb and emulate such as worked examples or diagrams.

What are the core ingredients?

DECONSTRUCT	VISUALISE	EXEMPLIFY
Break down complex tasks or concepts into smaller steps.	Combine explanation with visuals to represent concepts and ideas.	Compare and contrast successful and unsuccessful examples.

EXTERNALISE	SOLIDIFY	FADE
Reveal the thought process of an expert learner.	Provide tangible examples to make abstract ideas concrete.	Gradually remove support to develop student independence.

Related Summaries: Scaffolding (p.52), Worked Examples (p.56), Thinking Aloud (p.58)

How do I implement it?

Think aloud expert knowledge: Strategies such as thinking aloud help students understand the thought process of an expert learner. Think-alouds are most effective when implemented during the 'I do' phase of the learning process because they offer clear models of how and why experts select particular problem-solving methods.

BARAK ROSENSHINE

Students need cognitive support to help them learn to solve problems... modelling and thinking aloud... are examples of effective cognitive support. (2012)

Take small steps: In order to accommodate the limited capacity of working memory, modelling should involve presenting new information in small steps. This makes learning more manageable whilst increasing the chance of students making connections between their learning. Worked examples offer a practical method to achieve this.

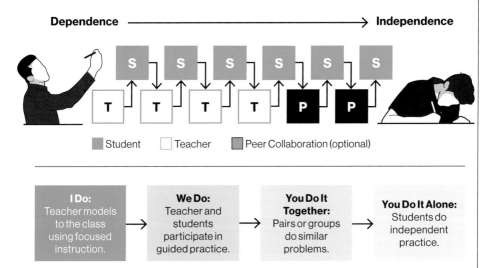

Dependence ⟶ Independence

S S S S S S

T T T T P P

■ Student ☐ Teacher ▨ Peer Collaboration (optional)

| I Do: Teacher models to the class using focused instruction. | We Do: Teacher and students participate in guided practice. | You Do It Together: Pairs or groups do similar problems. | You Do It Alone: Students do independent practice. |

Use the alternation strategy: During the 'I do' stage, use worked examples and think-alouds to externalise your approach. During the 'We do' stage, break problems into smaller chunks to give students a taste of success. Alternate between teacher modelling and the student practising each granular step. Only withdraw this support when there is a high enough success rate (around 80%).

Powerful Questioning

Prompt all students to think hard so that teachers can create regular opportunities to check depth of understanding

What is it and why is it important?

Our capacity to learn depends on our attention. In this context, the art of questioning is crucial in holding students accountable and checking their depth of understanding. Effective teachers recognise the importance of powerful questioning and cleverly weave a range of strategies into their instruction to test, deepen and develop students' understanding. As Tom Sherrington (2021b) elucidates, instead of asking students 'Do you understand?', teachers should craft questions that probe, 'What have you understood?'. This subtle shift helps teachers to make informed decisions on whether to move forward or revisit the material taught.

What are the core ingredients? (Chiles 2023a)

PITCH	PAUSE	NORMALISE
Pitch questions to prompt the right level of thinking.	Allow time for students to receive and process the question asked.	Normalise errors to create a healthy questioning culture.

GATHER	PROBE	PROMPT
Ask questions to a range of students to check understanding.	Ask follow up questions to extend thinking and check understanding.	Front load questions with how you want students to respond.

Related Summaries: Cold Calling (p.84), Think, Pair, Share (p.86), Mini-Whiteboards (p.88)

How do I implement it?

Plan powerful questions in advance: Questions should be clear and well-phrased, avoiding ambiguity. Craft them carefully so that they precisely target the intended learning objectives. Doug Lemov (2021) advises to 'script the language you'll use before the lesson and rehearse the answers yourself'. This will help you recognise a good answer and support with subsequent probing questions.

MICHAEL CHILES

Questioning is a staple feature of a teacher's toolkit... but of all the pedagogy strategies at the teacher's disposal, questioning is one of the most dominant methods of instruction. It is the heartbeat of a classroom. (2023b)

Give thinking time:
Provide adequate thinking time by posing questions and giving students a silent opportunity to reflect and formulate their responses without putting their hands up or discussing it with a peer.

THINKING TIME...

allows more hands to go up

gets higher quality answers

prompts more cognitive work

Follow up low level answers: Ask questions to help students improve.

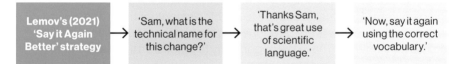

Lemov's (2021) 'Say it Again Better' strategy → 'Sam, what is the technical name for this change?' → 'Thanks Sam, that's great use of scientific language.' → 'Now, say it again using the correct vocabulary.'

Probe students by asking more questions: Always strive for a better answer. If students respond with 'I don't know', try and support them by asking more questions. Probing questions should be designed to encourage students to dig deeper so they have to think harder. For example: 'What is the main idea of ...?', 'Which one is the best ... why?', 'How does X compare to Y?'.

Collect responses from all students: Use tools like mini-whiteboards to quickly gather data on your students' understanding. Pose a question, provide time for students to think about their answer and write it down. Use a familiar prompt (such as '3, 2, 1, show me!') and actively scan responses. Give actionable feedback as you interact with students' answers in real time.

| Principle 1 | Principle 2 | Principle 3 | Principle 4 | **Principle 5** | Principle 6 |

Deliberate Practice

Provide extended opportunities for students to build skills so that they can gradually move from guided to independent work

What is it and why is it important?

The most effective teachers dedicate a substantial amount of time to deliberate practice. Deliberate practice is purposeful and focused effort to enhance performance in a particular skill over time. Additionally, guided practice involves collaborative efforts between teachers and students, using models, scaffolds and explanations to assist them in refining particular skills. As students develop proficiency in these skills, scaffolding and teacher intervention are gradually reduced to enable a smoother transition toward independence. Experts are developed through extensive practice and it is crucial for students to have the opportunity to practise in the classroom so that skills and knowledge become automatic.

What are the core ingredients? (Chiles 2023a)

CHUNK	TIME	NORMALISE
Chunk practice tasks taking into account cognitive load.	Plan sufficient time for students to practise applying knowledge.	Create a culture of healthy struggle where students learn to fail.

STRUCTURE	RECALL	LAYER
Provide clear guidance and show what success looks like.	Give opportunities for students to recall knowledge.	Increase complexity of practice as students develop schema.

Related Summaries: Retrieval Practice (p.104) Spacing and Interleaving (p.110), On-Task Time (p.152)

How do I implement it?

Start with guided practice and fade supports as students get better.

GUIDED PRACTICE (We do it)	Students show understanding	INDEPENDENT PRACTICE (You do it)

Fade physical, verbal and visual prompts.

Tell, then ask, and finally remind students what to do as they practice.

Practise without prompts or guidance.

Set similar tasks one at a time, check answers and give feedback.

Use the 30-40-30 rule during guided practice:
Provide several examples for all students to do:

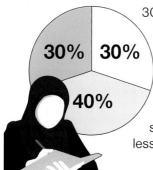

30% **30%** **40%**

30% of examples being doable at a basic level (start here).

40% of examples should be aimed at the 'core' level.

30% of examples should be challenging (after the successful completion of the less difficult examples).

DANIEL WILLINGHAM

It is virtually impossible to become proficient at a mental task without extended practice. (2010)

Create timely feedback loops:
In deliberate practice, feedback is essential for improvement. Just like one-on-one attention from a personal trainer or coach is highly effective, it is about pinpointing granular skills to improve and giving students time to develop them further. This means tasks should be designed to be shorter in length and focused on enhancing a specific area.

Space out practice tests:
According to John Dunlosky's (2013) research in 'Strengthening the Student Toolbox', practice testing and distributed practice are the most effective learning strategies. Getting students to retrieve answers from memory and spacing these practice sessions over time allows students time to master underlying skills and concepts.

| Principle 1 | Principle 2 | Principle 3 | Principle 4 | Principle 5 | **Principle 6** |

Feedback to Feedforward

Give actionable feedback and provide time for students to respond so that they can improve and move forward

What is it and why is it important?

Feedback is essential in moving learning forward. It can be delivered by teachers or peers and may be in an oral, written, formative, or summative form. Formative feedback is particularly impactful, providing concrete steps for learners to follow to help them achieve a specific goal and address learning gaps. Comment-only feedback that students can act upon is a powerful ingredient in students' learning diet. However, Dylan Wiliam's 'four quarters' marking approach – comprising 25% detailed feedback, 25% whole class feedback, 25% peer assessment and 25% self-assessment – offers an effective strategy for this purpose.

What are the core ingredients? (Chiles 2023a)

FEEDFORWARD	RECEPTIVE	GRANULAR
Feedback should focus on moving the learning forward.	Frame feedback to motivate students and build their confidence.	Create clear and concise action steps for students to act upon.

SELF-REGULATORY	ACTIONABLE	TIMELY
Use metacognitive strategies to help students self-regulate.	Provide students with something to do to improve themselves.	Time feedback according to the task or assessment at hand.

Related Summaries: Formative Assessment (p.80), Whole Class Feedback (p.92), Peer Critique (p.94)

How do I implement it?

5 Rs make feedback actionable: Actionable feedback is a powerful way for students to learn from their mistakes. Tom Sherrington (2017) notes that 'it ensures that they are able to do something very specific and concrete to improve their learning'. By employing the 5 Rs method, students actively engage with feedback, revisiting their work to refine specific skills or make targeted improvements.

DYLAN WILIAM

Feedback should be more work for the recipient than the donor. (2017b)

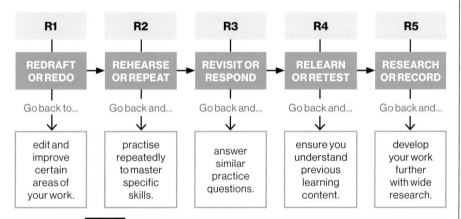

R1	R2	R3	R4	R5
REDRAFT OR REDO	**REHEARSE OR REPEAT**	**REVISIT OR RESPOND**	**RELEARN OR RETEST**	**RESEARCH OR RECORD**
Go back to...	Go back and...	Go back and...	Go back and...	Go back and...
edit and improve certain areas of your work.	practise repeatedly to master specific skills.	answer similar practice questions.	ensure you understand previous learning content.	develop your work further with wide research.

Turn feedback into detective work: Rather than thinking about feedback as information, think about feedback as detective work. Dylan Wiliam proposes that feedback should present a puzzle or challenge for the students to engage in. By framing it as an invitation to respond to the feedback, it makes it far more likely that students respond positively to the feedback (Barton 2022b).

Implement peer feedback: Model this process by showing students how to give effective feedback to others. Begin by giving feedback to anonymous pieces of work, and support the process with sentence starters or by having students write their comments on post-it notes.

Encourage the use of 'kind', 'specific' and 'helpful' language to promote a healthy feedback culture and ensure they have time to act upon their feedback. Subsequently, dedicate time for students to act upon their feedback and make improvements in class.

Summary

To do the best for our students and enable them to flourish, it is a school's obligation to build a solid foundation of pedagogical practice. Allison and Tharby (2015) advocate that their six principles should be infused in everything a school does: they should drive the curriculum, assessment, behaviour, leading colleagues, interactions with students and even the way leaders and teachers organise the school building. Not only are the principles in this collection evidence-informed, but also there is an underlying thread of hard work, motivation and aspiration to achieve excellence. These elements are explored in the next section. For now, here's a concise overview of the Expert Teaching Principles neatly captured in six statements of intent.

Principle 1: Incremental challenge

Expect excellence from all students and make learning desirably difficult so that everyone thinks hard and strives to achieve their best.

Principle 2: Precise explanation

Artfully weave new information into existing knowledge with clarity and precision so that students can build connected bodies of knowledge.

Principle 3: Layered modelling

Externalise thinking and show what success looks like in small steps so that students know how to apply new knowledge.

Principle 4: Powerful questioning

Prompt all students to think hard so that teachers can create regular opportunities to check depth of understanding.

Principle 5: Deliberate practice

Provide extended opportunities for students to build skills so that they can gradually move from guided to independent work.

Principle 6: Feedback to feedforward

Give actionable feedback and provide time for students to respond so that they can improve and move forward.

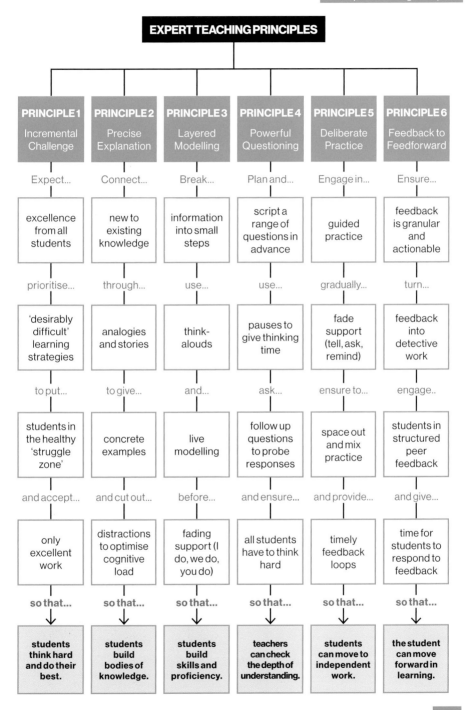

EXPERT TEACHING PRINCIPLES

PRINCIPLE 1	PRINCIPLE 2	PRINCIPLE 3	PRINCIPLE 4	PRINCIPLE 5	PRINCIPLE 6
Incremental Challenge	Precise Explanation	Layered Modelling	Powerful Questioning	Deliberate Practice	Feedback to Feedforward
Expect...	Connect...	Break...	Plan and...	Engage in...	Ensure...
excellence from all students	new to existing knowledge	information into small steps	script a range of questions in advance	guided practice	feedback is granular and actionable
prioritise...	through...	use...	use...	gradually...	turn...
'desirably difficult' learning strategies	analogies and stories	think-alouds	pauses to give thinking time	fade support (tell, ask, remind)	feedback into detective work
to put...	to give...	and...	ask...	ensure to...	engage..
students in the healthy 'struggle zone'	concrete examples	live modelling	follow up questions to probe responses	space out and mix practice	students in structured peer feedback
and accept...	and cut out...	before...	and ensure...	and provide...	and give...
only excellent work	distractions to optimise cognitive load	fading support (I do, we do, you do)	all students have to think hard	timely feedback loops	time for students to respond to feedback
so that...	so that...	so that...	so that...	so that...	so that...
students think hard and do their best.	**students build bodies of knowledge.**	**students build skills and proficiency.**	**teachers can check the depth of understanding.**	**students can move to independent work.**	**the student can move forward in learning.**

Classroom Culture:
A collection of one-pagers summarising strategies and ideas that achieve a positive classroom culture.

Teaching one Pagers

Classroom Culture

Culture is how we act based on what we believe

KATHARINE BIRBALSINGH

A teacher provides the child with structure and scaffolding to strengthen him so that he can fly. Children may be born with wings, but they need teachers to show them how to fly. (2020)

Culture is how we act based on what we believe. For a learning environment to feel safe and focused, there must be an underlying set of beliefs and core values that everyone understands and openly embraces.

It is the responsibility of school leaders to develop a clear vision and to shape the daily routines and norms for their students and teachers. Subsequently, teachers must uphold and consistently apply the agreed upon principles to ensure the school operates as one. Singing from the same hymn sheet is a must! Getting this right at the chalk face is also critical. All teachers know that noisy and uncontrolled classrooms and corridors impede learning and lead to frustratingly unpredictable learning environments.

Michaela Community School in Wembley Park, an underprivileged area of north London, is known widely across the UK as the 'strictest school in Britain' due to its high expectations and robust behaviour routines. Headmistress Katharine Birbalsingh has created a culture where students have clear boundaries, high standards and an intrinsic sense of belonging. The school was featured in the 2022 documentary *Britain's Strictest Headmistress* where Birbalsingh offers her blueprint for a better future by presenting twelve rules for radical educational change. You'll find these rules on page 142.

There are a few of Birbalsingh's rules I agree with. For example, as we discussed earlier, teachers must lead the learning (Rule 7) and empower students to build bodies of connected knowledge by explicitly teaching them new information from the front. As we know from cognitive science, this can be done through various evidence-informed instructional practices explored in **Collection 2: Expert Teaching Principles** which involve explaining, modelling and practising.

In my early career, explaining to students what they needed to know was seen as a cardinal sin. Back in the early 2010s, Ofsted considered excessive 'teacher talk' as limiting to students' learning as they were being denied independence and opportunities to collaborate with their peers. It used to make me feel guilty (and frustrated) explaining concepts in detail, as if I were somehow hindering their ability to discover and learn on their own. This perspective was part of a broader educational philosophy emphasising student-centred learning, where the teacher's role was more about facilitating and guiding rather than directly instructing. Whilst providing autonomy is crucial, I have discovered that a structured, teacher-led classroom forges high expectations and establishes a culture of accountability and respect.

Birbalsingh's first rule is that teachers must be the authority in the classroom and provide clear structure and behavioural boundaries that make the environment predictable, running like a well-oiled machine. As Birbalsingh writes in *Michaela: The Power of Culture* (2020), 'A teacher provides the child with structure and scaffolding to strengthen him so that he can fly. Children may be born with wings, but they need teachers to show them how to fly.' In other words, it's a teacher's professional duty to teach students routines and build positive habits to help them flourish.

TOM BENNETT OBE

Routines are the building blocks of classroom culture. (2020)

DOUG LEMOV

Perhaps the single most powerful way to bring efficiency, focus and rigor to a classroom is by installing strong procedures and routines. You define a right way to do recurring tasks; you practice doing them with students so they roll like clockwork. (2019)

'Britain's Strictest Headmistress' Rules

Rule 1: Adults must have authority
The teacher is the authority in the classroom which means they scaffold behaviour with clear structure and boundaries.

Rule 2: Gratitude needs to be taught
Teach students to be grateful for what they have and provide opportunities for them to show appreciation for others.

Rule 3: Insist on high standards
Keep standards high and hold the line by refusing to accept excuses and encouraging students to take responsibility for their actions.

Rule 4: Don't indulge a victim mentality
Motivate students by allowing them to struggle and give them the drive to take control of their own future.

Rule 5: Bin the smart phones
Encourage 'digital detox' by offering students the chance to hand in their smart phones to provide more focus on learning.

Rule 6: It's time to change the record
Encourage students to avoid poor role models and negative social influences so that they have high expectations of themselves.

Rule 7: Adults must lead the learning
As the expert in the classroom, the teacher's role is to explicitly tell students the information to build the knowledge they need to succeed.

Rule 8: Moral environment is crucial
Develop students' characters by consistently promoting high standards in politeness, punctuality and respect.

Rule 9: Provide a sense of national belonging
Build a sense of belonging by celebrating national identity in order to unite students and provide a sense of solidarity.

Rule 10: Dead white men still matter
Expose students to classic literature such as Shakespeare and Keats to provide them with a sense of national culture.

Rule 11: Encourage healthy competition
Provide students with the skills of resilience and strategy by exposing them to healthy competition with each other.

Rule 12: Strict works when wrapped in love
Teachers hold students to account because they show that they care and push them to be the best they can be.

Ryan and Deci (2020) showed that cultivating these conditions leads to an increase in intrinsic motivation because students discover a sense of autonomy (feeling in control of their academic actions), competence (believing effort will lead to growth) and relatedness (feeling a sense of belonging in class). Establishing a consistent and predictable classroom environment can largely be achieved through one key element: the implementation of routines.

In his book *Running the Room*, Tom Bennett explains that 'routines are the building blocks of classroom culture' and writes that 'routine behaviour must be taught not told'. Classroom routines are like cogs in a machine. Each routine, no matter how small, functions like a cog, playing a crucial role in the smooth and efficient operation of the classroom. When these routines are established and consistently followed, they mesh together seamlessly, creating a cohesive and functional learning environment. Teaching routines step-by-step and rehearsing them with a class is fundamental to ensuring the machine runs smoothly. Doug Lemov captures the powerful impact of routines perfectly. He writes (2019), 'Perhaps the single most powerful way to bring efficiency, focus and rigour to a classroom is by installing strong procedures and routines.' He goes on to explain how practice is key to making routines habitual: 'You define a right way to do recurring tasks; you practice doing them with students so they roll like clockwork.'

Since introducing instructional coaching at my school, I have had the privilege of working with lots of teachers to help shape and improve particular aspects of their teaching. Using the instructional coaching platform Steplab has raised my awareness of the importance of rehearsal in forming positive habits that foster positive long-term change. Rehearsal and deliberate practice are essential tools in embedding routines for students too. By repeatedly practising routines, students internalise them, making their execution almost automatic. These habits make the classroom far more fluid, predictable and far less interrupted!

The following one-pagers offer nudges and conversation prompts for establishing routines and developing high expectations in your classroom or school. Before digging into the one-pagers in this section, take a moment to read the summary of Tom Bennett's *Running the Room* on the next page. Afterwards, do yourself a favour and purchase a copy to find out more! You won't regret it.

Running the Room

The Teacher's Guide to Behaviour

TOM BENNETT OBE

Being well-behaved is a combination of skills, aptitudes, habits, inclinations, values and knowledge. These can be taught.
(2020)

What is the book about and why is it important?

Tom Bennett's book *Running the Room* (2020) is a practical guide for teachers on getting good behaviour in classrooms. Bennett's stance is that all teachers can improve in 'running the room' if they are trained well. The book sets up the one-pagers in this collection beautifully because it outlines how we can explicitly teach behaviour (like any academic subject) and not simply tell students to behave. Bennett highlights the importance of establishing norms and building solid routines. The summaries that follow reinforce Bennett's beliefs that 'better behaviour is essential to good learning' and offer strategies and routines that teachers can implement to establish positive classroom habits to optimise learning.

What main ideas are introduced?

Teach (don't just tell) them how to behave: As the adult in the classroom, teachers must teach behaviour, *not* react to it. Since not all students know how to behave, we must prevent the likelihood of behavioural issues occurring by planning to deal with the most common problems. Drive standards by removing obstacles in order to help students form better habits and be sure to challenge low-standards every time. This will lead to a healthy, learning focused classroom.

Entry Routines

Activity Transitions

Class Dismissal

Corridor Conduct

Tracking

Silence

Read More: *Running the Room: The Teacher's Guide To Behaviour* by Tom Bennett

How do I teach behaviour and build habits?

Teach behaviour as you would teach the curriculum: Not all students understand what good behaviour means or have observed what it looks like. The behaviour curriculum must be taught, similar to how we would teach an academic or practical subject. Teachers can do this by using instructional practices such as modelling, providing opportunities for practice, checking for understanding and giving feedback. Training students using Rosenshine's principles of instruction as a framework can support with teaching good behaviour and building lasting routines.

DESIGN	DESCRIBE	DEMONSTRATE	DEMAND	DISENGAGE
Decide the routines you want and need	Agree on how you will tell students about them	Get students to practise the routine repeatedly	Make sure students perform it each time	Let students do the routine without cues

Establish norms and practice routines: Classroom norms make it easy for students to behave and difficult for them not to. Norms foster a sense of belonging and involve teaching and demonstrating the values you want to see. Routines are sequences of specific behaviours that 'are the building blocks of classroom culture' (Bennett 2020). They include actions such as entry to the classroom, transitions between activities and answering questions. Regular practice of routines helps to internalise expectations. The three main factors for changing habits are: repetition, providing cues and a balance of extrinsic and intrinsic rewards to build motivation.

Plan, script and practice:

Improving any behaviour takes practice. Having a script creates the impression that you are calm, prepared and focused. Consistency is the foundation of all habits. Practise using scripts so that phrases and instructions become habitual. Habits persist only as long as they are practised. As soon as we stop practising, we start to lose them.

Provide behaviour feedback:

Whenever a student behaves in a certain way, their environment should offer cues about he appropriateness of their behaviour. Implementing consequences as part of a feedback loop helps to influence students' future behaviour. Consistently offer both extrinsic rewards and sanctions for inadequate behaviour.

Classroom Culture

Excellent Work

Focus on the learning process, not the final result

RON BERGER

Work of excellence is transformational. Once a student sees that he or she is capable of excellence, that student is never quite the same. (2003)

What is it and why is it important?

Ron Berger has gained widespread recognition for his book *An Ethic of Excellence* and his presentation on the story of Austin's Butterfly. Berger advocates that producing excellent work can bring about transformational changes. He presents the idea that once students recognise their capability for excellence, they strive for nothing less. Berger's approach emphasises the importance of high-quality work and setting high expectations to encourage students to aim for excellence. Focusing on the process of learning, rather than solely on the end result, helps students to become resilient in the face of challenges. It also helps students gain from collaboration and peer feedback.

What are some of the main takeaways from Berger's work?

1	Teach students how to give kind, specific and helpful feedback.
2	Spend more time on the crafting and drafting process.
3	Offer independent practice on similar tasks to consolidate learning.
4	Embrace mistakes and emphasise the process not the outcome.
5	Make work public so others can see success and give feedback.

Read More: *An Ethic of Excellence: Building a Culture of Craftsmanship with Students* by Ron Berger

How do I implement this?

Utilise models to show examples of excellence:
Quality modelling offers students a clear example of excellence that they can visualise and carry with them. Models provide students with something concrete which they can use to support and construct their own thinking. Modelling and externalising your cognitive strategies through think-alouds helps students to develop their own metacognitive skills.

SONIA THOMPSON

It is about taking students' work beyond the singular audience and into a world where there is now even more a reason to care about its quality. (2022)

Dedicate time for multiple drafts: Berger (2003) asks the question: 'What kind of quality work can you create in just one draft?' He suggests that students must understand from the beginning that producing high-quality work involves reviewing, revising and refining. Achieving excellence requires numerous cycles of iterative refinement. Dedicate time for students to revisit and improve their work based on your feedback or critique from peers.

'I really liked it when...'

'Try to include more..'

'Develop your use of...'

'In paragraph one...'

Employ peer critique: The peer critique process helps students realise that their knowledge is not fixed but rather, it evolves over time. Berger's method to peer critique helps students to internalise the criteria for success and give their peers kind, specific and helpful feedback so that they can make incremental adjustments to their work to enhance learning.

Publicly share work: Sharing student work creates a sense of accountability and encourages them to produce high-quality work that they can be proud of. Producing work for an authentic audience can inspire and motivate them to push themselves even further. Seeing examples of success helps students set higher goals for themselves and work towards achieving them.

Classroom Culture

Lesson Planning

Plan and optimise successful learning sequences

What is it and why is it important?

Professor Robert Coe's 'poor proxies for learning', highlights how ineffective planning can lead to a focus on activity design and keeping students busy as opposed to learning. Lesson planning should concentrate on what teachers intend for students to learn over time, acknowledging that learning emerges from repeated, iterative exposures to material within a scheme of work. Effective planning involves mapping out, chunking down and thinking about how the elements of the learning sequence are linked together. Peps Mccrea's (2015) 'Lean Framework' presents four key questions to ask when planning effective lessons.

> How can I best help them get there?
>
> ↑
>
> How will I know when they're there?
>
> ↑
>
> Where do I want them to go?
>
> ↑
>
> Where are my learners starting from?

DOUG LEMOV

Eschew the complex if something less clever, less cutting-edge, less artfully constructed will yield a better result. (2011)

How do I implement this?

Optimise instruction: During lesson planning, make sure you fully understand the content and boil it down to the key learning points you want students to know. Streamlining information helps teachers to write clear learning objectives and establish clear success criteria. Scripting precise explanations and questions before the lesson is an effective way to ensure clarity and promote thinking. Rehearsing these elements before the lesson is beneficial. Additionally, consider the activities you want students to engage in and allocate a specific time limit for each.

Read More: *Lean Lesson Planning* by Peps Mccrea

Forming a learning objective: Learning objectives should be specific and describe what the learner will be able to do. Avoid generalised terms such as *know* and *understand* and instead use specific words like *match, describe* and *compare*. Visualising a learning journey with an end point and steps along the way also makes it easier in identifying what children need to contemplate or practise in any one lesson. For instance, a visual arts teacher might map out the following sequence:

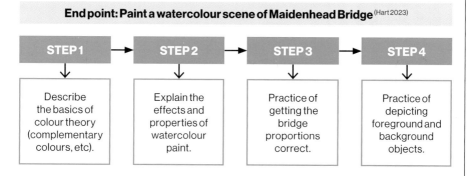

End point: Paint a watercolour scene of Maidenhead Bridge (Hart 2023)

STEP 1	STEP 2	STEP 3	STEP 4
Describe the basics of colour theory (complementary colours, etc).	Explain the effects and properties of watercolour paint.	Practice of getting the bridge proportions correct.	Practice of depicting foreground and background objects.

Take the shortest path: Doug Lemov's 'the shortest path' involves getting into the habit of asking yourself: 'What is the minimum my students (or I) need to do to help them learn X?' Essentially, when taking the shortest path, the goal is to get as many students to the goal as possible in the shortest time. This means removing complexity or unnecessary elements in lessons to free up students' working memory and focus only on what's important.

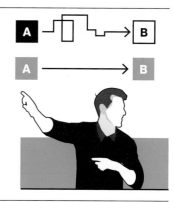

Develop habits of thought:
Principal Nick Hart (2023) states 'deciding what we want children to learn and the work that they will do to make that happen is the bread and butter of teaching'. Hart's questions prove invaluable for teachers in formulating effective lesson plans.

1 'What do I want students to learn in this learning sequence?'

2 'What task will directly help them to progress towards this goal?'

3 'Does the task match the objective? What will they be thinking about?'

Classroom Culture

Establishing Routines

Create a predictable, learning-focused environment

CAROL ANN TOMLINSON

Classroom routines... allow teaching and learning to proceed in a structured, predictable and efficient manner. (2010)

What are they and why are they important?

Classroom routines are taught procedures that are carried out by teachers and students, aimed at fostering a safe and learning-focused environment. For example, a routine might be for students to get out mini-whiteboards at the start of a lesson so they are ready to use when needed. Classroom routines are important because they shape a structured environment where students can learn effectively. Routines make the classroom predictable so students know what to expect in any given lesson. Automating these classroom procedures means that more time can be spent on learning.

How do I implement them?

Establish the routines: Routines varies based on the age of students you teach. Clear guidelines should be determined for the regular operations that set students up for success. For example, having students line up outside the room, beginning class with a 'Do Now' activity, preparing learning materials in advance, and setting acceptable noise levels for productive learning.

Entering

Noise Levels

Timers

Transitions

'Do Now'

Read More: *Leading and Managing a Differentiated Classroom* by Carol Ann Tomlinson

Clarify the rationale for the routines: To ensure students understand why routines are established, provide them with the general rationale and explain how the routine is beneficial. For example, 'In this class, we keep noise levels at an appropriate level so that we can all concentrate and learn without being distracted.'

MARK DOWLEY

In short, behaviour itself is a curriculum. We must remember teaching behaviour is the same as teaching any other curriculum. We must transfer! (et al 2024)

Explicitly teach the routines: Avoid merely giving students a list of procedures and assuming they will understand them. Educators and authors Mark Dowley and Ollie Lovell (2024) explain that 'teaching behaviour is the same as teaching any other curriculum'. They propose teachers can transfer effective methods of instruction to teaching behaviour. Explicitly planning, scripting, teaching and modelling behavioural routines provides a concrete examples of what success looks like.

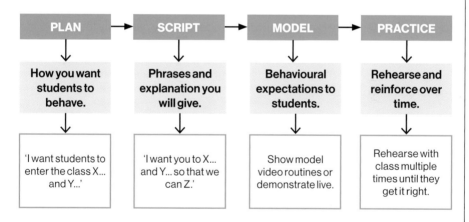

PLAN	SCRIPT	MODEL	PRACTICE
How you want students to behave.	Phrases and explanation you will give.	Behavioural expectations to students.	Rehearse and reinforce over time.
'I want students to enter the class X… and Y…'	'I want you to X… and Y… so that we can Z.'	Show model video routines or demonstrate live.	Rehearse with class multiple times until they get it right.

Apply and automate routines: Get students to begin using the routines. Circulate the classroom and ask students to recall the reason for why a specific routine has been implemented. Ask them the steps required and what it should look and sound like.

Reflect, revise and review: Monitor students as they engage in a routine. Consider: 'Is this routine contributing to a positive teaching and learning environment?' Revise procedures if they do not work and be sure to review them every so often.

Classroom Culture

On-Task Time

Direct, support and monitor independent work

What is it and why is it important?

Part of a positive classroom culture involves providing on-task time that encourages students to get 'into the zone' and fully focus on the learning at hand. Getting students fully absorbed independently in cognitively demanding work and extended practice is challenging and can sometimes seem unachievable. Studies indicate that when activities aren't independent (or quiet), students are likely to learn less because they can't fully focus and process new information. With clear structure, support and shared goals we can optimise instructional attention. Implementing effective strategies for independent, focused learning requires intentional planning and consistent reinforcement of classroom norms.

How do I implement it?

Carefully design seating arrangements:

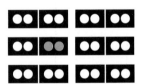

Simmons et al (2015) suggest that teachers who want to optimise on-task behaviour during independent work should consider using rows rather than groups as their primary seating arrangement. As we know, without attention, learning is less likely to take place. Using rows decreases the chance of students getting distracted by their peers or extraneous information in the learning environment. Additionally, research shows that horseshoe-shaped seating plans are an effective choice for both independent work and class discussion as (most) students are facing each other and the teacher.

Read More: *Teaching Walkthrus* by Tom Sherrington and Oliver Caviglioli

Set a challenging short-term goal: As Dylan Wiliam (2011) notes: 'If you don't know where you're going, you'll never get there.' This is true not only for learning intentions of the lesson but task intentions. Describe the task clearly and make the steps concrete. Visualise each step by displaying them on the board: 'Step 1: Predict (verb) what will happen to Lady Macbeth (context) in Act 5, Scene 5 (content). Duration: 10 minutes.'

Strategically circulate the room: Circulation involves moving strategically around the classroom to engage with students to personally support their learning. Before the lesson, plan the route you are going to take around the room during on-task time. The planned route should cover every student, ensuring that you are as responsive as possible to all your students. Signal first what you will be looking out for during circulation and record misconceptions.

Set timers: Use timers to designate specific time periods for activities during on-task time. This can help students manage their time more effectively and encourage them to stay on task. Before introducing a timer, be sure to communicate the purpose of it first: 'Alright, everyone, we're going to start our group activity now, and I'll be setting a timer for 15 minutes. The purpose of the timer is to help us stay focused.'

MARY MYATT

With practice comes proficiency which is the highway to the long-term memory... there is no shame in getting things wrong because, with practice, that is how we learn. (2019)

Working in silence: When students are on-task and engaged in independent generative learning, silence is incredibly powerful. A quiet learning environment fosters calmness and focus and sets a comfortable tone for hard thinking. As with any routine, silence needs to be explicitly taught and rehearsed. Set specific time-limits for each episode of silence and stick to the rules yourself to model success. This means you must resist the urge to break the silence by speaking to students as they are working.

Classroom Culture

Transitions

Streamline routines to maximise learning time

What are they and why are they effective?

A classroom transition is the process of smoothly moving students from one activity or setting to another. There are three main types of transitions: entering class, switching from one activity to another and exiting class. And just like any instructional procedure, transitions should be taught through explicit explanations, models and rehearsal. Students need practice because it is easy to lose focus between class transitions. As transitions become more routine and automatic, behavioural issues decrease, allowing more time to be allocated to learning.

TOM BENNETT OBE

Routines are the building blocks of the classroom culture. Routine behaviour must be taught not told. (2020)

How do I implement them?

Plan and script transitions: Decide on a transition that requires improvement. For instance, preparing or packing away mini-whiteboards, or beginning a writing task. Deconstruct the parts of this transition into bite-size instructions and write them out:

1	'OK, it's time to use your mini-whiteboards. First, take your whiteboard and pen out of the folder.'
2	'You have 10 seconds to place your pen and board on top of your work. Well done, X.'
3	'Now, remember to start writing when I say the action word which is '3, 2, 1 – show me'.'

Teach the transition: Michael Linsin (2015) explains that teachers can standardise the time between each lesson or activity so it runs predictably smoothly. He sets out five key steps in building successful transitions:

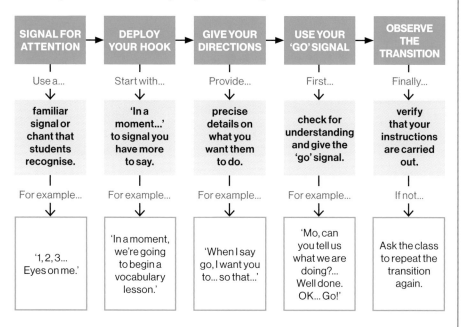

SIGNAL FOR ATTENTION	DEPLOY YOUR HOOK	GIVE YOUR DIRECTIONS	USE YOUR 'GO' SIGNAL	OBSERVE THE TRANSITION
Use a...	Start with...	Provide...	First...	Finally...
familiar signal or chant that students recognise.	'In a moment...' to signal you have more to say.	precise details on what you want them to do.	check for understanding and give the 'go' signal.	verify that your instructions are carried out.
For example...	For example...	For example...	For example...	If not...
'1, 2, 3... Eyes on me.'	'In a moment, we're going to begin a vocabulary lesson.'	'When I say go, I want you to... so that...'	'Mo, can you tell us what we are doing?... Well done. OK... Go!'	Ask the class to repeat the transition again.

Model the transition: In order to be proficient at a specific transition, successful models are essential. This could involve creating video examples with colleagues or personally demonstrating the transition. Engage with the class to discuss the effectiveness of the model and co-create a checklist of success criteria.

Rehearse with the class:
Multiple rounds of rehearsal allows students to see and feel what it is like to do the transition. Offer feedback and narrate the positives when students are carrying it out: 'Well done Sam, you have done X brilliantly!'.

Set clear time frames: Set time parameters for students to carry out the transition: 'You have 30 seconds to get...'. Use reminders of time remaining: '10 seconds left'. Do not be afraid to get students to start from scratch if the transition is unsuccessful.

Group Work

Establish group goals and provide accountability

What is it and why is it effective?

Typically, group work involves students collaborating, often in small groups, to jointly understand, solve problems, or create something based on information they have just learned. Group work should only be used if it enhances learning outcomes, otherwise individual or peer activities will work better. When introducing collaborative activities, it is critical that it is set up with structure and clear goal-setting in mind. Dylan Wiliam (Education Scotland 2016) explains that collaborative learning is only effective when group goals and individual accountability is established.

DYLAN WILIAM

Collaborative learning works in the classroom when you have group goals and individual accountability. (Education Scotland 2016)

How do I implement it?

Set clear goals for group work: Ensure that students have defined objectives to achieve throughout the group work process. If the goal spans over several lessons, develop a timeline of expectations and checkpoints for students to follow. Learning objectives need to be precise and describe what the learners will be able to do. Steer clear of vague terms such as 'know' and 'understand', instead use specific words like 'match', 'describe' and 'compare' (Bangerter et al 2020). For instance: 'Learners will predict (verb) the outcome of an experiment (context) on the solubility of common materials in water (content).'

Watch: Education Scotland YouTube Video: 'Dylan Wiliam: Collaborative Learning'

Ensure accountability: It's crucial for teachers to assign specific roles to students within their groups. This will ensure the group dynamics work and will minimise personality clashes between students. Outline the specific roles for the task with a brief description of the key responsibilities.

FACILITATOR	REFLECTOR
Keeps the conversation focused on the learning objective oversees time management.	Guides consensus-building process for the group: 'Would you all agree that... is a good answer for...?'

NOTETAKER	DEVIL'S ADVOCATE
Records the main discussion points and summarise the main actions or overall agreements.	Raises counter-arguments and introduces alternative explanations and possible ideas.

Make all students accountable: When defining group roles, avoid assigning a 'reporter'. This responsibility only holds only the designated individual accountable for feeding back the group's ideas to the class. Similar to the 'Cold Calling' questioning strategy, group work should engage students in listening, thinking and being ready to respond. A useful idea to help with these steps is a contract. Develop a signed agreement outlining what students are expected to achieve, the responsibilities of each group member (who is going to do what) and specific deadlines.

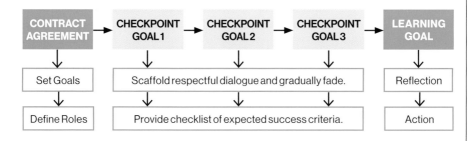

CONTRACT AGREEMENT	CHECKPOINT GOAL 1	CHECKPOINT GOAL 2	CHECKPOINT GOAL 3	LEARNING GOAL
Set Goals	Scaffold respectful dialogue and gradually fade.			Reflection
Define Roles	Provide checklist of expected success criteria.			Action

Scaffold respectful dialogue: Model effective communication and respectful language by actively listening to your students and demonstrating how to acknowledge others' viewpoints. Offer sentence starters to scaffold the group discussion, ensuring that students communicate respectfully and do not interrupt: 'Could you clarify the point about...?', 'I respect your viewpoint but I disagree with...', 'I'd like to build on Grace's idea...'.

Classroom Culture

Great Homework

Blend a range of Mode A and Mode B activities

TOM SHERRINGTON

There is the need to provide a diet of homework that blends different opportunities and purposes. (2019b)

What is it and why is it important?

Homework is vital in helping students practise and learn independently. Sherrington's Mode A and Mode B formula (2019b) is a powerful way to strike a balance between instructional practices that help build knowledge and fluency with more open-ended, creative approaches. Research indicates that more specific and precise homework has a greater impact on all learners. Setting a high volume of great homework helps students improve planning and regulate their learning – an important factor in the EEF's metacognition and self-regulation report (Quigley et al 2018).

How do I implement it?

Mode A
Refers to...
↓
practice and consolidation activities.
This means...
↓
you explain... you model... they practise... check and give feedback... test them... and again later.

Mode B
Refers to...
↓
open-ended response activities.
This means students...
↓
explore... discover... hands-on experiences... inspire some awe... go off piste... projects... choice.

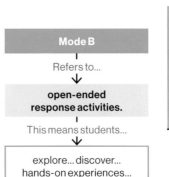

80% Mode A

20% Mode B

Decide on a Mode A and Mode B split for your own school context.

Read More: *The Learning Rainforest: Great Teaching in Real Classrooms* by Tom Sherrington

Give lots of Mode A homework:

Mode A learning involves activities that give students opportunities to practise and consolidate their learning. As Sherrington explains, lesson time is not enough on its own for deep learning. Therefore, structured guidance to help build fluency is crucial. Prioritise and set more Mode A homework for your students and get them consolidating their learning.

Give some Mode B homework:

Mode B learning is about allowing students the freedom to express creativity and explore areas of the curriculum in self-directed ways. This work should be open-ended but still include some teacher input and structure. Set Mode B homework sparingly and decide with your team the diet of homework you believe will maximise learning.

MODE A ACTIVITIES

Routine Questions: Fluency building questions with built-in self assessment opportunities.

Knowledge Retrieval: Flashcard revision, online quizzes, labelling diagrams, mind-map activities.

Pre-Study: Learning vocabulary, pre-reading, flipped learning tasks, paragraph writing exercises.

MODE B ACTIVITIES

Research Projects: Leave responses open but provide structure by giving clear objectives.

Creative Choices: Explore curriculum topics by offering choices to present new learning.

Oracy: Plan or record a speech, debate, persuasive argument about a topic.

Scaffold respectful dialogue:

Decide (with your team) on a sensible Mode A/Mode B split. It should be manageable and sustainable. As Sherrington explains (2019b), 'If either you automatically associate setting more homework with having more marking *or* you dismiss the amount of learning that can happen outside of your lessons, then you're doing it wrong!'

Make assessment easy:

Great homework should not cause excessive workload. Set tasks that can be self-assessed or given simple teacher validation. For example, Mode A work can be reviewed and self-assessed at the beginning of a lesson. For Mode B homework, it might be that you dedicate a lesson to peer critique and scaffold kind, specific and helpful comments.

Classroom Culture

Behaviour Management

Establish a positive and respectful learning environment

BILL ROGERS

Whenever we discipline a student in the busy ebb and flow of a classroom, we are not merely addressing that student; it is also a social transaction. (2015)

What is it and why is it important?

Dr Bill Rogers' behaviour management principles emphasise the importance of effective communication and conflict resolution. These principles include keeping language as least intrusive as possible to avoid confrontation (unless absolutely necessary) and maintaining an assertive, respectful and positive tone in all interactions with students. Rogers' approach focuses on building positive relationships with students and developing clear expectations and consequences. Explicitly addressing and de-escalating poor behaviour demonstrates a zero-tolerance stance. On-the-spot strategies are vital for establishing a positive classroom environment conducive to deep learning.

How do I implement them?

Utilise positive corrective language: It is the teacher's role to communicate a sense of calmness, order and focus. Instead of making requests or demands, it is better to describe what we observe and direct the expected behaviour positively. For example, saying calmly: 'A number of students are talking (descriptive cue of the observed behaviour). Settling down now, everyone. Thanks (positive language to mitigate potential escalation).' This approach not only reduces confrontation but also builds a positive and respectful classroom atmosphere.

Read More: *The Classroom Management Handbook* by Mark Dowley and Ollie Lovell

BE LEARNING FOCUSED	OFFER DIRECTED CHOICE	REFER TO SCHOOL POLICY
Start by saying...	Next, say...	Finally explain...
↓	↓	↓
'How's the task going Ethan? Can I help you to get you started?'	'About that phone. Either put it in your bag OR put it on my desk. Thanks.'	'The school's policy with mobile phones is that they must be away at all times.'

Offer directed choices: First, check in with the student and enquire about their work before calmly giving a clear directed choice. Offering a choice about the consequences helps to defuse potential conflicts. Refer to the school's behaviour guidelines and tactically ignore negative reactions, unless they are serious. For more serious behaviours, be assertive and expect compliance without relying solely on punitive measures.

Tactically ignore (only when necessary): Young people are often insecure in social settings, which can lead to behaviours such as eye rolling and sighing. Rogers classifies these examples as 'secondary behaviours' that can be tactically ignored, as they are often not the primary issue. More serious behaviours should always be addressed and subsequent time should be taken to follow up with a student to repair and rebuild the relationship before their return to class.

Chewing gum in the bin. Thanks.

Your tone is rude and unacceptable.

Allow take up time: Address the primary behaviour and afford the student time to reflect by diverting your gaze from them. Tactically ignore any negative reactions that may arise, unless they are serious. If the behaviour persists, clarify the consequence. For example: 'If you choose not to do X, I will address this at the end of the lesson.'

Partially agree: Partial agreement is a useful way to stop unnecessary arguments (secondary behaviours) from taking over. This strategy involves using two words: 'maybe' and 'but'. For instance, acknowledge the student by saying, 'Maybe you aren't distracted; however, I need you two to work silently.'

Classroom Culture

Teacher Presence

Lead the learning with confidence and authority

What is it and why is it important?

Classroom presence refers to the way in which you conduct yourself in your classroom to show authority. This includes your use of body language, tone of voice and overall demeanor. Positioning involves situational awareness and strategically moving or standing in different areas of the classroom to maximise learning. Developing classroom presence and teacher positioning strategies can foster a sense of control, structure and respect in your classroom. Refining these strategies additionally, aids in building relationships with students, potentially leading to more positive and productive learning experiences for everyone.

TOM BENNETT OBE

Children need an adult presence, they need an adult sense of authority in the room. It's your right to run the room. (2020)

How do I implement this?

Build your classroom radar: Doug Lemov (2021) discusses strategies that allow teachers to see student behaviour more comprehensively. For instance, 'The Swivel' technique from *Teach Like a Champion* entails deliberately scanning the classroom regularly. The 'Be Seen Looking' technique ensures students aware that you can see them by exaggerating non-verbal cues to direct their behaviour. Regular practise of these strategies will convey control to your students and show them that you can see their behaviour and that it matters.

Look

Raise Eyebrow

Gesture

Nod

Read More: *Running the Room: The Teacher's Guide to Behaviour* by Tom Bennett

80°

Utilising Pastore's Perch: In *Teach Like a Champion*, Lemov (2021) discusses the strategy of using 'Pastore's Perch' to position yourself effectively so that you can see all students in your field of view. This spot is generally located in the corner of the room, rather than the centre, and enables you to monitor if students are on task. As students are working, assess when to circulate around the room for intervention and when to return to your perch for observation.

Face the class during circulation: When students are on-task, move around the classroom scanning for signs of on-task or off-task behaviour. As you move around, make sure to position yourself to face the class, enabling you to spot any unwanted behaviour. Engage in brief, unobtrusive conversations with students about their work and offer the right amount of support. When interacting with students, avoid turning your back to the class.

Develop non-verbal strategies: Employ low-key behaviour management strategies to give the message that you can see their non-compliance. For instance, this could include using facial expressions, nodding your head, lightly tapping on a student's desk, or raising an eyebrow. These strategies are unobtrusive and do not draw everyone's attention to the behaviour so learning can continue without disruption. These gentle signals create a respectful and focused classroom atmosphere.

Project confidence: Even if you are feeling differently on the inside, use a variety of verbal and non-verbal techniques to present control.

EYE CONTACT
Scan the room before focusing on an individual.

↓

PACE
Speak slowly and practise using pregnant pauses to maintain attention.

↓

BODY LANGUAGE
Chest proud, hands apart, feet apart and leaning back slightly.

↓

VOICE
Lower your voice so that it comes from your chest not your head.

↓

LANGUAGE
Be firm, positive but always expect compliance.

Effective Praise

Build students' intrinsic motivation and self-efficacy

What is it and why is it important?

Praise involves acknowledging students' efforts and offering constructive feedback. Without it, the classroom environment runs the risk of becoming clinical and impersonal. Genuine praise can motivate struggling students and validate those who are more successful. Moreover, precise praise focused on the learning at hand positively impacts and increases student motivation. When praise is delivered effectively, it strengthens students' beliefs in their abilities. Carol Dweck famously explains that offering praise for effort cultivates a growth mindset in students, which lets them know that hard work pays off. Furthermore, when praise is used regularly, you tend to have better relationships with your students, enjoy more instructional time, and see fewer behavior problems.

CAROL DWECK

Praising children's intelligence harms their motivation and it harms their performance.
(2007)

How do I implement it?

Praise students' efforts not just performance: Focus on commending students' effort rather than solely their performance. This involves recognising hard work and praising specifically what students can control: 'I am so impressed at how hard you worked to improve this paragraph.' This is more empowering than 'you are a great writer', as this implies a fixed ability that did not involve hard work.

'You worked hard to include...'

'I'm impressed with your crafting of...'

'I can see you improved your...'

Read More: *Mindset: Changing The Way You Think to Fulfil Your Potential* by Carol Dweck

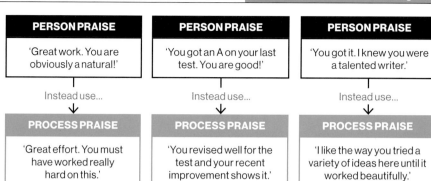

PERSON PRAISE	PERSON PRAISE	PERSON PRAISE
'Great work. You are obviously a natural!'	'You got an A on your last test. You are good!'	'You got it. I knew you were a talented writer.'
Instead use...	Instead use...	Instead use...
PROCESS PRAISE	PROCESS PRAISE	PROCESS PRAISE
'Great effort. You must have worked really hard on this.'	'You revised well for the test and your recent improvement shows it.'	'I like the way you tried a variety of ideas here until it worked beautifully.'

Praise the process not just the outcome: In addition to praising effort, it's crucial to acknowledge students' achievements throughout a learning sequence to reinforce that the process and strategies they use are just as important as reaching their goal. For instance: 'The strategy you used in section two was excellent because...'. This will support students' metacognitive skills and encourage them to monitor their own learning.

Utilise behaviour-specific praise (BSP): Specific praise involves using descriptive language to prompt students into thinking about the next steps in their learning or behaviour. Avoid general compliments like 'good work'. Instead, use behaviour-specific praise. Illustrate the positives with concrete examples, such as: 'You listened carefully to your partner, Ava.'

Differentiate between public and private praise: Most students benefit from praise, but not all students need the same kind. Burnett (2001) revealed that primary school age students often appreciate being complimented publicly, while adolescents prefer private praise. In class, be conscious of how individual students react to public or private praise.

Use sincere and specific language: In their research, Brummelman et al (2013) found that giving inflated praise – in particular to those students who have low self-esteem – is well intentioned but can backfire. It can damage your relationship with the student and cause them to avoid crucial learning experiences – a process that may eventually undermine their learning and performance. Instead, it is recommended to use simple 'I' statements to communicate sincere appreciation: 'I always look forward to hearing your ideas, Alex.'

Motivation

Establish trust and cultivate a culture of success

What is it and why is it important?

In his book, *Motivated Teaching*, Peps Mccrea explains that 'Motivation influences behaviour, learning and wellbeing'. Ultimately, a lack of motivation leads to student disengagement and apathy. Teachers should establish routines that create opportunities for students to experience success as often as possible because achievement serves as a catalyst for even more accomplishments. It is paramount to nurture a culture where high student success is celebrated and learning to embrace failure is encouraged. Motivation emerges from a sense of belonging that can be achieved by establishing a safe and trusting classroom environment.

PRITESH RAICHURA

Building motivation is a long-term project, ultimately amplified by building strong relationships with students. (2023b)

How do I implement this?

Establish trust by positively framing interactions: Intrinsic motivation can be built through classroom interactions. Instead of using praise alone, it is useful to give a range of useful and honest feedback and guidance that includes both praise and critical or corrective feedback (Lemov 2021). Do this by:

- 'Assuming the best' in students' academic efforts, not the worst.

- Focusing on the next step to success (do not dwell on what went wrong but what you want to see).

- Narrating the positive behaviours by recognising and describing them as they happen.

Read More: *Motivated Teaching* by Peps Mccrea

Cultivate the conditions for success: Research shows that creating learning environments where students feel autonomy, competence and relatedness helps students to build and maintain intrinsic motivation (Ryan et al 2020).

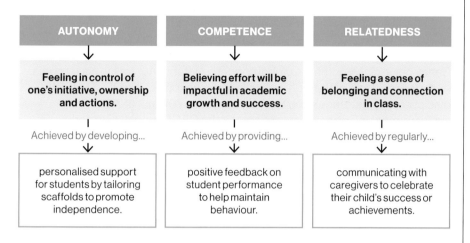

AUTONOMY	COMPETENCE	RELATEDNESS
↓	↓	↓
Feeling in control of one's initiative, ownership and actions.	Believing effort will be impactful in academic growth and success.	Feeling a sense of belonging and connection in class.
Achieved by developing... ↓	Achieved by providing... ↓	Achieved by regularly... ↓
personalised support for students by tailoring scaffolds to promote independence.	positive feedback on student performance to help maintain behaviour.	communicating with caregivers to celebrate their child's success or achievements.

Ensure and celebrate high success rates: In Barak Rosenshine's 'Principles of Instruction', he suggests that the optimal success rate a teacher should aim for is 80%. To boost their confidence and competence, foster a culture where students are celebrated for their successes so that they can draw upon these experiences in future.

Use extrinsic rewards sparingly: Reward systems are an effective way in which teachers can celebrate student success and effort. Token rewards like postcards home or lottery tickets provide extrinsic motivation for students. As Mccrea (2023) explains: 'sometimes we need to deploy "extrinsic motivators" to get the ball rolling'. Extrinsic motivation works best when we:

1 Give to celebrate rather than to coerce. Catch students being good and avoid using 'If-Then' incentives: 'If you do X, then you'll get Y'.

2 Clearly link to the desired behaviour by being specific every time... 'a merit for including the key term in your answer'.

3 Apply the reward as soon as possible. Have a clipboard with a seating plan to hand and (visibly) note it down there and then.

Summary

Behaviour in classrooms is a global concern. Notably, Australian classrooms experiences some of the highest levels of disruption. As the OECD's (2018) disciplinary climate index shows, Australia ranks 70th out of 77 school systems, meaning classrooms are among the OECD's most disorderly. However, this concerning situation does have potential for improvement, and there is light glimmering at the end of the tunnel!

Safe, orderly and positive learning environments are the bedrock for learning. In other words, learning is as successful as the culture, expectations, routines and rules taught to and reinforced with students. To create calm and ordered classrooms where learning takes priority, explicitly teaching behaviour, routines and establishing high expectations is a must. Tom Bennett's work on this highlights the importance of instilling positive – not punitive – strategies to build belonging, responsibility and motivation. Here are some key takeaways from Collection 3.

Takeaway 1: Teach routines

Explicitly teach, model and rehearse behavioural routines so that students form positive habits that aid their learning.

Takeaway 2: Optimise instruction

Optimise instruction and design well-structured lessons so that students pay attention and are less likely to be disengaged.

Takeaway 3: Set high expectations

Consistently uphold high expectations so that students purposefully craft, draft and produce excellent work.

Takeaway 4: Build intrinsic motivation

Praise effort and create opportunities for success so that students feel in control, believe in their academic abilities and experience a sense of belonging.

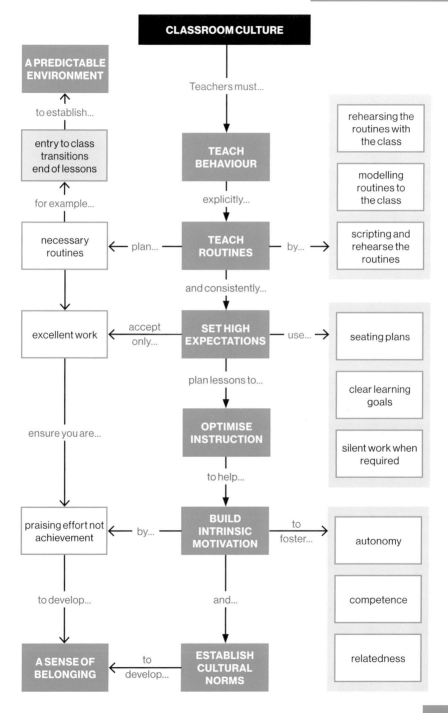

Read More:

A reference list of studies, books and blogs that inspired and influenced the collections in this book.

Read More

Adegbuyi, F. and Todoist Website. (No date). 'How to Learn Anything with the Feynman Technique: Why teaching is the key to understanding. https://todoist.com/inspiration/feynman-technique.

Agarwal, P. K., Roediger, III, H. L., McDaniel, M. A. and McDermott, K. B. (2020). 'How To Use Retrieval Practice To Improve Learning', retrievalpractice.org, Washington University in St Louis.

Allison, S. and Tharby, A. (2015). *Making Every Lesson Count: Six Principles to Support Great Teaching and Learning.* Crown House Publishing.

Archer, A. L. (2010). *Explicit Instruction: Effective and Efficient Teaching.* Guilford Press.

Atherton, A. (2021). 'Defining Excellence: How I Use Whole Class Feedback', 15 July [Blog] codexterous. https://codexterous.home.blog/2021/07/15/defining-excellence-how-i-use-whole-class-feedback/.

Atkins, R. (2023). *The Art of Explanation: How to Communicate with Clarity and Confidence.* Wildfire.

Ausubel, D. (1963). *The Psychology of Meaningful Verbal Learning.* Grune & Stratton.

Ausubel, D. P., Novak, J. D. and Hanesian, H. (1978). *Educational Psychology: A Cognitive View* (2nd edition). Holt, Rinehart and Winston.

Bangerter, M., Trebilco, J. (2020). 'Three Ingredients for Better Learning Outcomes', 15 January [Blog] Monash University. https://www.monash.edu/learning-teaching/news/blog/ingredients-for-better-learning-outcomes.

Barton, C. (Host). (March 2022a). Adam Boxer [Audio podcast episode]. In Tips for Teachers podcast. Spotify. https://open.spotify.com/episode/6N63IX5tzDYTv8RKLbXIyy?si=5d0d8ed68f1e4ea4.

Barton, C. (Host). (March 2022b). Dylan Wiliam [Audio podcast episode]. In Tips for Teachers podcast. Spotify. https://open.spotify.com/episode/2DTECaymncMIqpxaeNbtfH?si=cKuM33weQNG7Znuh8Wea_A.

Bennett, T. (2020). *Running the Room: The Teacher's Guide to Behaviour.* John Catt Educational.

Berger, R. (2003). *An Ethic Excellence Grade 3-8: Building A Culture of Craftsmanship With Students.* Pearson.

Birbalsingh, K. (2020). *Michaela: The Power of Culture.* John Catt Educational.

Bjork, E. L. and Bjork, R. A. (2011). 'Making things hard on yourself, but in a good way: Creating desirable difficulties to enhance learning', in M. A. Gernsbacher, R. W. Pew, L. M. Hough and J. R. Pomerantz (eds.), *Psychology and the real world: Essays illustrating fundamental contributions to society* (2nd edition). (pp. 59–68). New York: Worth.

Bjork, E. L. and Bjork, R. A. (1994). 'Making Things Hard on Yourself, But in a Good Way: Creating Desirable Difficulties to Enhance Learning'. https://www.researchgate.net/publication/284097727_Making_things_hard_on_yourself_but_in_a_good_way_Creating_desirable_difficulties_to_enhance_learning.

Brummelman, E., Thomaes, S., Orobio de Castro, B. and Overbeek, G. (2014). '"That's Not Just Beautiful-That's Incredibly Beautiful!" The Adverse Impact of Inflated Praise on Children With Low Self-Esteem', *Psychological Science*, 25(3), 728–735.

Burnett, P. C. (2001). 'Elementary Students' Preferences for Teacher Praise', *The Journal of Classroom Interaction,* 36(1), 16–23.

Busch, B. and InnerDrive. (No date). 7 Approaches to Using AI in the Classroom (With Prompts). https://blog.innerdrive.co.uk/7-approaches-to-ai.

Carpenter, S. K. and Agarwal, P. K. (2020). 'How To Use Spaced Retrieval Practice To Boost Learning'. http://pdf.retrievalpractice.org/SpacingGuide.pdf.

Caviglioli, O. (2019). *Dual Coding with Teachers*. John Catt Educational.

Caviglioli, O. and Goodwin, D. (2021). *Organise Ideas: Thinking by Hand, Extending the Mind*. John Catt Educational.

Centre for Education Statistics and Evaluation. (2017). 'Cognitive load theory: Research that teachers really need to understand', New South Wales Government.

Chase, C. C., Chin, D. B., Oppezzo, M. A. and Schwartz, D. L. (2009). 'Teachable Agents and the Protege Effect: Increasing the Effort Towards Learning', *Journal of Science Education and Technology*, 18, 334–352.

Chiles, M. (28 August 2023a). (@m_chiles). 'The Quality of Education is built on a core set of principles [emoji] We will work together to narrate what each principle looks like in the classroom using our components and active ingredients [emoji] @coopbellevue @SFL2326 @atcha_ms', 28 August [Tweet], https://x.com/m_chiles/status/1696037060631535817?s=20.

Chiles, M. (2023b). *Powerful Questioning Strategies for Improving Learning and Retention in the Classroom*. Crown House Publishing.

Christodoulou, D. (2019). 'The No More Marking: Whole-Class Feedback: A Recipe, Not a Statement', 28 March [Blog] The No More Marking Blog. https://blog.nomoremarking.com/whole-class-feedback-a-recipe-not-a-statement-e2a6704ea434.

Clark, R. (2009). 'Give your Training a Visual Boost', 23 April [Online] Association for Talent Development. https://www.td.org/magazines/give-your-training-a-visual-boost.

Clark, J. and Chohan, A. (2022). 'Showbie: Considerations for Creating and Implementing an Effective Feedback Policy'

Clear, J. (2018). *Atomic Habits: An Easy & Proven Way to Build Good Habits & Break Bad Ones*. Avery.

Coe, R. (2013). Improving Education: A triumph of hope over experience. Inaugural Lecture of Professor Robert Coe, Durham University, 18 June 2013.

Coe, R. (2015). 'Centre for Evaluating and Monitoring, What Makes Great Teaching?'. IB World Regional Conference (AEM) [Presentation], 31 October.

Coe, R., Higgins, S. and Major, L. E. (2014). 'What makes great teaching?' https://my.chartered.college/early-career-hub/what-makes-great-teaching/.

Collin, J., Smith, E. and Education Endowment Foundation. (2021). Effective Professional Development: Guidance Report. Education Endowment Foundation.

Cottingham, S. (12 April 2023a). (@SCottinghatt). 'Here's a one-pager of implications of Ausubel's work – thank you @XpatEducator for making it! I'm speaking at @researchEDWarr & @rEDBerks on *Ausubel's Meaningful Learning* - do joint to learn more. Here are a few things in the meantime... [Image attached]', [Tweet] 12 April, https://twitter.com/SCottinghatt/status/1646140543095787520?s=20.

Cottingham, S. (12 April 2023b). (@SCottinghatt). '(1) Bodies of knowledge are the *goal* We don't want students who can parrot back individual bits of information. We want students who have developed *bodies of connected knowledge* (think a vast complex network of assimilated ideas)...', [Tweet] 12 April, https://x.com/SCottinghatt/status/1646140548581867521?s=20.

Cottingham, S. (2023c). *Ausubel's Meaningful Learning in Action*. John Catt Educational.

D'Mello, S., Lehman, B., Pekrun, R. and Graesser, A. (2014). 'Confusion can be beneficial for learning', *Learning and Instruction*, 29, 153–170.

Dowley, M. and Lovell, O. (2024). *The Classroom Management Handbook: A Practical Blueprint for Engagement and Behaviour in Your Classroom and Beyond*. John Catt Educational.

Dunlosky, J. (2013). 'Strengthening the Student Toolbox: Study Strategies to Boost Learning', *American Educator*, Fall, pp. 12–21.

Dunlosky, J., Rawson, K. A., Marsh, E. J., Nathan, M. J. and Willingham, D. (2015). 'What Works, What Doesn't', 1 January [Online] Scientific American. https://www.scientificamerican.com/article/what-works-what-doesn-t/.

Dweck, C. (2007). *Mindset: The New Psychology of Success*. Random House Publishing Group

Education Endowment Foundation. (2021a). Using Digital Technology to Improve Learning. Guidance Report. https://educationendowmentfoundation.org.uk/education-evidence/guidance-reports/digital.

Education Endowment Foundation. (2021b). Feedback. https://educationendowmentfoundation.org.uk/education-evidence/teaching-learning-toolkit/feedback.

Education Endowment Foundation. (2021c). Metacognition and Self-Regulated Learning. Guidance Report. https://educationendowmentfoundation.org.uk/education-evidence/guidance-reports/metacognition.

Education Scotland. (2016). 'Dylan Wiliam: Collaborative learning'. YouTube Video. Retrieved from: https://youtu.be/TqBNWEQmBRM?si=vt_UGo7PgBnixmx_

Enser, M. and Enser, Z. (2020). *Fiorella & Mayer's Generative Learning in Action*. John Catt Educational.

Fiorella, L. (2023). 'Making Sense of Generative Learning', *Educational Psychology Review*, 35(2), 1–42.

Fletcher-Wood, H. (2013). 'Do they understand this well enough to move on? Introducing hinge questions', 17 August [Blog] Improving Teaching. https://improvingteaching.co.uk/2013/08/17/do-they-understand-this-well-enough-to-move-on-introducing-hinge-questions/

Fletcher-Wood, H. (2019). 'Exit Tickets: Encapsulating Tasks and Retention', 16 June [Blog] Improving Teaching. https://improvingteaching.co.uk/2019/06/16/exit-tickets-responsive-teaching-2019-update-encapsulating-tasks-and-retention/.

gocognitive. (13 July 2012). robert bjork – using our memory shapes our memory [Video]. YouTube. https://www.youtube.com/watch?v=69VPjsgm-E0.

Hart. N. (2023). 'LO: write learning objectives and success criteria'. Blog. Retrieved from: https://mrnickhart.wordpress.com/2023/10/06/lo-write-learning-objectives-and-success-criteria/.

InnerDrive. (No date a). 'The Importance of Think, Pair, Share (And How To Do It Properly)'. https://blog.innerdrive.co.uk/how-to-use-think-pair-share

InnerDrive. (No date b). 'The 6 Benefits Of Retrieval Practice – A Visual Guide'. https://blog.innerdrive.co.uk/6-benefits-of-retrieval-practice.

InnerDrive. (No date c). 'Why Daily, Weekly and Monthly Reviews Matter'. https://blog.innerdrive.co.uk/daily-weekly-monthly-review.

Jones, K. (2019). *Retrieval Practice: Resources and Research For Every Classroom.* John Catt Educational.

Knight, J. (2021). *The Definitive Guide to Instructional Coaching: Seven Factors for Success.* ASCD.

Kirschner, P., Sweller, J. and Clark, R. (2006). 'Why minimal guidance during instruction does not work: An analysis of the failure of constructivist, discovery, problem-based, experiential and inquiry-based teaching', *Educational Psychologist,* 41(2), pp. 75–86.

Lemov, D. (2010). *Teach Like A Champion: 49 Techniques That Put Students On The Path To College (K–12).* John Wiley & Sons.

Lemov, D. (2011). *Teach Like a Champion, Enhanced Edition: 49 Techniques that Put Students on the Path to College (K-12).* John Wiley & Sons.

Lemov, D. (2019). 'A case study in the power of academic procedures and routines.'. Doug Lemov's Field Notes. Retrieved from: https://teachlikeachampion.org/blog/a-case-study-in-the-power-of-academic-procedures-and-routines/

Lemov, D. (2021). *Teach Like a Champion 3.0: 63 Techniques that Put Students on the Path to College.* Jossey-Bass.

Linsin, M. (2015). 'The Secret To Perfect Transitions In 5 Simple Steps', 17 January [Blog] Smart Classroom Management. https://smartclassroommanagement.com/2015/01/17/the-secret-to-perfect-transitions-in-5-simple-steps/.

Lovell, O. (2021). *Sweller's Cognitive Load Theory in Action.* John Catt Educational.

Marzano, R. J. (2010). 'The Art and Science of Teaching/Representing Knowledge Nonlinguistically', 1 May [Online] ASCD.

Mayer, R. (2005a). 'Introduction to Multimedia Learning' in R. E. Mayer, *The Cambridge Handbook of Multimedia Learning.* Cambridge University Press, p. 1.

Mayer, R. (2005b). 'Cognitive Theory of Multimedia Learning' in R. E. Mayer, *The Cambridge Handbook of Multimedia Learning.* Cambridge University Press, pp. 43–71.

Mccrea, P. (2015). *Lean Lesson Planning: A practical approach to doing less and achieving more in the classroom.* CreateSpace.

Mccrea, P. (2017). *Memorable Teaching: Leveraging Memory to Build Deep and Durable Learning in the Classroom.* CreateSpace.

Mccrea, P. (2020a). 'The Gatekeeper to Thinking: Attention', 30 March [Blog] Active Learning Trust. https://activelearningtrust.org/blog/2020-03-30-16-02-21-the-gatekeeper-to-thinking-attention.

Mccrea, P. (2020b). *Motivated Teaching: Harnessing the science of motivation to boost attention and effort in the classroom.* CreateSpace.

Mccrea, P. (2023). 'Evidence Snacks: Eliminate Potential Distractions: Reducing Extraneous Load in the Classroom', 16 March [Blog] Pepsmccrea.com. https://snacks.pepsmccrea.com/p/eliminate-potential-distractions.

Myatt, M. (2019). *The Curriculum: Gallimaufry to Coherence.* John Catt Educational.

Nuthall, G. (2007). The Hidden Lives of Learners. New Zealand: Research and Development Division, NZCER Press.

OECD (2018). PISA 2018 Results (Volume III): What School Life Means for Students' Lives. https://www.oecd-ilibrary.org/sites/f05bb3ee-en/index.html?itemId=/content/component/f05bb3ee-en

Ofsted (Office for Standards in Education, Children's Services and Skills). General guidance on teaching methodologies and classroom practices in the UK.

Quigley, A. (2018). 'Huntington Research School: Making Sense of Metacognition', 27 April [Blog] Huntington Research School. https://researchschool.org.uk/huntington/news/making-sense-of-metacognition.

Quigley, A., Muijs, D. and Stringer, E. (2018). 'Metacognition and Self-Regulated Learning: Guidance Report'. Education Endowment Foundation. www.bit.ly/3u6zual.

Raichura, P. (2023a). 'The Three Phases of Questioning', Bunsen Blue [Blog] 22 April. https://bunsenblue.wordpress.com/2023/04/22/the-three-phases-of-questioning/.

Raichura, P. (2023b). 'Cultivating enthusiasm'. Blog. Retrieved from: https://edu.rsc.org/ideas/7-ways-to-motivate-your-students/4017342.article.

Rogers, B. (2015). *Classroom Behaviour: A Practical Guide to Effective Teaching, Behaviour Management and Colleague Support (4th Edition).* Sage Publications.

Rosenshine, B. (2012). 'Principles of Instruction: Research-Based Strategies That All Teachers Should Know', *American Educator* (Spring), 12–39.

Rosenthal, R. and Jacobson, L. (1968). 'Pygmalion in the Classroom', *The Urban Review*, 3, 16–20.

Ryan, R. M. and Deci E. L. (2020). 'Intrinsic and extrinsic motivation from a self-determination theory perspective: Definitions, theory, practices, and future directions', Contemporary Educational Psychology, 61.

Simmons, K., Carpenter, L., Crenshaw, S., Hinton, V. M. (2015). 'Exploration of Classroom Seating Arrangement and Student Behavior in a Second Grade Classroom', *Georgia Educational Researcher*, 12(1), 51–68.

Shank, P. (2021). *Write Better Multiple-Choice Questions to Assess Learning: Measure What Matters—Evidence-Informed Tactics for Multiple-Choice Questions.* Independently published.

Sherrington, T. (2014). 'The Progressive-Traditional Pedagogy Tree', 15 March [Blog] teacherhead. https://teacherhead.com/2014/03/15/the-progressive-traditional-pedagogy-tree/.

Sherrington, T. (2017). '#FiveWays of Giving Effective Feedback as Actions', 18 December [Blog] teacherhead. https://teacherhead.com/2017/12/18/fiveways-of-giving-effective-feedback-as-actions/.

Sherrington, T. (2018). 'Mode A + Mode B = Effective teaching and a rich enacted curriculum.' 22 April [Blog] teacherhead. https://teacherhead.com/2018/04/22/mode-a-mode-b-effective-teaching-and-a-rich-enacted-curriculum/.

Sherrington, T. (2019a). '10 Techniques for Retrieval Practice', 3 March [Blog] teacherhead. https://teacherhead.com/2019/03/03/10-techniques-for-retrieval-practice/.

Sherrington, T. (2019b). 'Setting Great Homework: The Mode A:Mode B Approach'. Blog. Retrieved from: https://teacherhead.com/2019/03/11/setting-great-homework-the-mode-amode-b-approach/.

Sherrington, T. (2020). 'A model for the learning process. And why it helps to have one', 10 March [Blog] teacherhead. https://teacherhead.com/2020/03/10/a-model-for-the-learning-process-and-why-it-helps-to-have-one/.

Sherrington, T. (2021a). 'Cold Calling: The #1 strategy for inclusive classrooms – remote and in person.', 7 February [Blog] teacherhead. https://teacherhead.com/2021/02/07/cold-calling-the-1-strategy-for-inclusive-classrooms-remote-and-in-person/.

Sherrington, T. (2021b). 'Check for Understanding... why it matters and how to do it. #rEDSurrey21' Blog. Retrieved from: https://teacherhead.com/2021/10/17/check-for-understanding-why-it-matters-and-how-to-do-it-redsurrey21/.

Shimamura, A. (2018). *MARGE: A Whole-Brain Learning Approach for Students and Teachers.* CreateSpace.

Sumeracki, M. (2019). 'Retrieval Practice: Hiding Broccoli in the Brownies', July [Blog] The Learning Scientists. https://www.learningscientists.org/blog/2018/7/19-1.

Sweller, J. (1988). 'Cognitive load during problem solving: Effects on learning', *Cognitive Science*, 12(2), 257–285.

Sweller, J., Ayres, P. and Kalyuga, S. (2011). *Cognitive Load Theory.* New York Springer.

Sweller, J., van Merriënboer, J. J. G. and Paas, F. (2019). 'Cognitive Architecture and Instructional Design: 20 Years Later', *Educational Psychology Review*, 31(2), pp. 261–292.

Tayler, L. and Lemov, D. (2021). 'A Graphic Representation of Timing the Name In Cold Call', 24 August [Blog] Teach Like A Champion. https://teachlikeachampion.org/blog/a-graphic-representation-of-timing-the-name-in-cold-call/.

TED. (2007, 7 Jan). Do schools kill creativity? | Sir Ken Robinson. [Video]. YouTube. https://youtu.be/iG9CE55wbtY?si=y_Fao9Tk9b9x5HnW.

Thompson, S. (2022). *Berger's An Ethic of Excellece in Action.* John Catt Educational.

Tomlinson, C. A. and Imbeau, M. B. (2010). *Leading and Managing a Differentiated Classroom.* Association for Supervision & Curriculum Development.

Weinstein, Y. and Sumeracki, M. (2016). 'The Learning Scientists.. 'Learn How to Study Using... Elaboration. Learn How to Study', July [Blog] The Learning Scientists. https://www.learningscientists.org/blog/2016/7/7-1.

Weinstein, Y., Madan, C. R. and Sumeracki, M. A. (2018). 'Teaching the science of learning', *Cognitive Research Principles and Implications*, 3(1), pp. 1–17.

Wiliam, D. (2011). *Embedded Formative Assessment.* Solution Tree Press

Wiliam, D. and Black, P. J. (1998). 'Inside the Black Box Raising Standards Through Classroom Assessment', September. https://www.researchgate.net/publication/44836144_Inside_the_Black_Box_Raising_Standards_Through_Classroom_Assessment.

Wiliam, D. (2000). 'Integrating formative and summative functions of assessment', King's College London.

Wiliam, D. and Leahy, S. (2015). *Embedding Formative Assessment: Practical Techniques for K-12 Classrooms.* Learning Sciences International.

Wiliam, D. (2017a). Embedded Formative Assessment (2nd edition). Solution Tree Press.

Wiliam, D. (26 Jan 2017b). (@dylanwiliam). 'I've come to the conclusion Sweller's Cognitive Load Theory is the single most important thing for teachers to know http://bit.ly/2kouLOq>', [Tweet] 26 Jan, https://twitter.com/dylanwiliam/status/824682504602943489.

Willingham, D. T. (2010). *Why Don't Students Like School?: A Cognitive Scientist Answers Questions About How the Mind Words and What It Means for the Classroom.* Jossey-Bass.

Willingham, D. T. (2021). 'How to Foster Creativity in Children', 13 April [Online] Worth. https://www.worth.com/how-to-foster-creativity-in-children.